Fermented Foo~~~ ~~~~
to Ferment Vegetables

by Morgan Anderson

Disclaimer:

This information is provided for consumer informational and educational purposes only and may not reflect the most current information available. This book is sold with the understanding the author and/or publisher is not giving medical advice, nor should the information contained in this book replace medical advice, nor is it intended to diagnose or treat any disease, illness or other medical condition. Always consult your medical practitioner before making any dietary changes or treating or attempting to treat any medical condition.

This information does not cover all possible uses, precautions, interactions or adverse effects of the topics covered in this book. Do not disregard, avoid, or delay seeking medical advice because of something you may have read in this book. Always consult your doctor before adding herbs to your diet or applying them using any of the methods described herein.

While we endeavor to keep the information up to date and correct, we make no representations or warranties of any kind, express or implied, about the completeness, accuracy, reliability, suitability or availability with respect to the book or the information, products, services, or related graphics contained book for any purpose. Any reliance you place on such information is therefore strictly at your own risk.

It's important that you use good judgment when it comes to fermented food. Do not consume food you think may have gone bad because it looks, smells or tastes bad. The author claims no responsibility for any liability, loss or damage caused as a result of use of the information found in this book.

Dedication:

This book is dedicated to all those who have discovered the many benefits of fermented food. I'd like to thank my friends and family, who were kind enough to taste-test the recipes for this book. Thanks guys! I couldn't have done it without you.

Contents

A Brief History of Fermentation

The fermentation process is a natural biological process that predates man. Fruits and vegetables alike begin to ferment when they fall off the vine and are left to sit for any period of time. The natural bacteria and yeasts found on their skins become part of a chain reaction that ultimately breaks the food down and returns it to the Earth. That is, if it isn't found by a foraging animal and consumed first.

It's suspected that human consumption of fermented food predates recorded history. It's probably safe to assume early humans who stumbled across naturally fermenting foods didn't turn their noses up at the thought of eating them. They likely consumed them and reaped the benefits of eating probiotic foods without ever realizing what they were doing.

What is known is that fermented foods have been a way of life for mankind for tens of thousands of years at a bare minimum. It isn't known what the first fermented foods were or when their benefits were discovered, but fermented food has been a part of the human diet as far back as one can look in documented history.

Fermenting preserves food and allows it to be stored for months or even years, as opposed to the short time most food will last if it's harvested and left to sit on the counter. Foods like milk products, fruits and vegetables were fermented to extend their shelf lives and to ensure our ancestors had food to eat when times got tough. Food preservation techniques like fermentation allowed people to move into areas with harsh winter environments because they allowed them to preserve the harvest and save food for the months when the weather turned cold, the ground hardened and the environment turned too hostile to grow crops in.

Pick a culture from anywhere around the globe and you'd be hard-pressed to find one that doesn't have a rich history of fermenting food. It's known that vegetables have been fermented for at least 6,000 years. The ancient Chinese lacto-fermented cabbage and served it to the groups of people tasked with building the Great Wall of China. Kimchi was fermented in Korea, kefir in Russia, sauerkraut in Germany, natto in Japan. There are literally hundreds of fermented foods that have traditionally been consumed by cultures spanning the globe.

In the last hundred years or so, Western cultures have largely made the switch from live-cultured foods full of probiotic bacteria to foods that have been processed to kill all bacteria, both good and bad. While getting rid of bad bacteria is a plus, this switch to dead foods has left our bodies severely lacking in the healthy probiotic cultures they need to thrive.

Fermented foods have seen a resurgence in modern times as people realize the many health benefits associated with them. Lactobacillus bacteria have been proven by scientific studies to be beneficial bacteria that play a major role in digestive health.

Fermented foods have played a crucial role in the diets of humans for tens of thousands of years. There's no good reason they shouldn't be a part of the diet of healthy individuals today.

The Lacto-Fermentation Process

Lacto-fermentation occurs when food is fermented using a special type of bacteria known as lactobacteria. There are a number of varieties of lactobacteria found in fermented foods, but the one thing they all have in common is they all produce lactic acid as a byproduct as they break food down into simple components. The fermentation process also produces small amounts of alcohol and a measurable amount of carbon dioxide.

When vegetables are harvested and placed in an anaerobic environment, the lactobacteria found naturally on the skins of the vegetables begin to process the vegetables. As the lactobacteria take control, they start converting simple carbohydrates into lactic acid. They emit carbon dioxide as a byproduct as they break the food being fermented down into simple units. These units are easily digested and processed into energy when fermented foods are consumed.

The lactic acid emitted by the lactobacteria preserves the food by preventing it from going bad. Harmful bacteria have trouble growing in the acidic environment created by lacto-fermentation, which means fermented foods can last indefinitely. Food will eventually be broken down to the point it is no longer palatable, but this takes much longer than it would take for the food to go bad if left to spoil of its own accord.

What You Need to Get Started

In order to safely lacto-ferment vegetables, you need four items:

- **Vegetables.**
- **Salt.**
- **Water.**
- **A fermenting vessel.**

Let's take a closer look at each of these items.

Vegetables

There isn't much to explain here.

Most vegetables can be fermented. The best vegetables for fermenting are usually vegetables that in prime eating condition. Vegetables that have started to go bad won't magically become edible again after fermentation. For this reason, it's important to plan ahead and to start fermenting vegetables a short time after they're harvested, as opposed until waiting until the last minute when they're starting to get soft.

Avoid using damaged vegetables with soft spots or bruised. If forced to use these vegetables, cut away any damaged areas before you ferment the vegetables. Vegetables that have rotten or moldy spots should never be used because they're already under attack by the wrong type of microorganisms.

Salt and Water

Salt and water are combined to create brine.

Salt is added to the water because harmful bacteria aren't able to survive in salty water, but lactobacteria can. By adding salt to the water used for fermentation, you create an environment conducive to the growth of beneficial bacteria. Without salt, the lactobacteria found naturally on the foods may wind up competing with harmful bacteria for resources.

Using a salty enough brine kills off the harmful bacteria before they can take hold, giving the beneficial bacteria free reign to reproduce and to process the food. As the bacteria create lactic acid, the lactic acid further prevents the growth of harmful bacteria.

A Fermenting Vessel

Lacto-fermentation is an anaerobic process, meaning it needs to take place in an environment devoid of oxygen. If oxygen is present, the wrong types of bacteria can start to grow in the container. For this reason, airtight containers are needed for fermenting.

There are two basic types of fermenting vessels to choose from. Airtight vessels prevent air from getting in or out of the container. Mason jars with airtight lids are an example of a simple airtight container. These containers will work in a pinch, but you have to be careful. Tremendous pressure can build up inside the containers due to the carbon dioxide created during the conversion of sugars into lactic acid. If this pressure isn't released, containers can explode or have their tops pop off. Exercise caution when opening airtight containers because the liquid inside the container can spray out and make a mess.

Fermenting vessels will be covered in-depth in a later chapter.

P 43 + P. 24 ON·····

The Health Benefits of Fermented Vegetables

Fermented vegetables have a long list of health benefits associated with them. The probiotic flora, digestive enzymes and vitamins and minerals found in fermented vegetables combine to create a food packed so full of nutritional value, it's tough to beat.

The following list contains some of the known health benefits of fermented vegetables:

- **They are rich in digestive enzymes.** The body needs enzymes to digest food and to absorb nutrients. Fermented foods replenish lost enzymes in the body and ensure the food you eat is properly digested. You get more nutrients from all of the food you eat when your gut contains an adequate level of digestive enzymes.

- **They are rich in probiotic bacteria.** The human body needs healthy amounts of good bacteria to function at a high level. These bacteria aid with digestion and help give the immune system a boost. Maintaining healthy levels of gut flora doesn't just aid with digestion, it keeps you healthier in general. Eating foods high in probiotic bacteria helps eliminate bad bacteria trying to take hold in the body.

- **Fermented foods are easier to digest and eating them aids the body with digestion.** The enzymes and bacteria in fermented foods help your body break down other food as it's taken in. Fermented foods are usually easier to digest than non-fermented foods because they've already been partially broken down into simple components.

- **Fermented foods aid with nutrient absorption.** You'll absorb more nutrients from the foods you eat when fermented foods are part of your diet.

- **Fermenting makes food healthier.** In addition to providing beneficial bacteria and enzymes, some fermented foods have been shown to have higher levels of certain vitamins after fermenting than they did before they were fermented. Vegetables are one of those foods.

- **Fermented foods are a quick source of energy.** If you're feeling run down and need a quick energy boost, fermented foods are already partially digested, so they'll give you a faster energy boost than most other foods.

Even though fermented foods have been around for thousands of years, scientists are just now realizing exactly how good these foods are for people. A number of studies are being done to study the effects of fermented foods on the human body and there's still much to be learned about the health value of fermented foods.

Stay tuned, as more and more studies are revealing previously unknown health benefits associated with fermented foods.

Vegetable Fermenting Basics

There are two schools of thought when it comes to fermenting vegetables.

Wild fermentation is the more natural of the two methods. Vegetables are placed in brine and are left to ferment of their own accord. The natural bacterium existing on and in the vegetables takes over and ferments them. It's fermentation in its most simple form, as it takes nothing more than vegetables, brine and a container.

Assisted fermentation takes place when some sort of starter culture is added to give the vegetables a gentle push in the right direction. The main difference between the two types of fermentation is starter cultures speed up the fermentation process. Starter cultures allow you greater control over the types of beneficial bacteria you get from your fermented foods because you choose the types you want to add.

Those who advocate wild fermentation over assisted fermentation believe wild fermented vegetables have a more robust bacterial composition than assisted fermentation. When you add cultures, the cultures you add are going to be the ones most likely to grow. You never quite know what you're going to get when you wild ferment vegetables, as you can't be sure exactly what lactobacteria will be present. While this may not sound like a benefit, the chances of getting a wider variety of lactobacteria are increased when you wild ferment vegetables, so they may be better for you.

The basic steps for vegetable fermentation are the same regardless of which method is used. The only difference is whether starter culture is or isn't added.

Here are the basic steps required to ferment vegetables:

1. **Wash the containers you plan on fermenting the vegetables in and the utensils you plan on using.** A simple cleansing with soap and hot water will suffice. Don't use antibacterial soap because it can have a negative effect on the beneficial bacteria in the fermented food. Thoroughly cleanse the utensils and the containers because harmful bacteria can be introduced into the process if dirty items are used. For smaller containers, you may just want to run them through the dishwasher with no soap added.

2. **Wash the vegetables.** Most vegetables can be washed under running water. Dirtier vegetables may need to be soaked and rinsed a couple times. Don't use too hot of water or you run the risk of killing the beneficial bacteria that exist naturally on the vegetables. If you do that, you're going to have to use starter culture.

3. **Process the vegetables.** This may involve blanching, peeling, steaming or any number of processing steps. It almost always involved chopping or cutting the vegetables into smaller pieces. The smaller the pieces, the easier it is to ferment the vegetables because more surface area is exposed to the brine.

4. **Add salt to the vegetables.** This will naturally draw moisture out of the vegetables. The salt will mix with the water and create a brine solution the vegetables can be fermented in.

5. **Place the vegetables in the fermenting vessel and let them sit for a while to release moisture.** Some vegetables need to be left to sit overnight to ensure enough moisture has been released to create an ample amount of brine to ferment the vegetables in.

6. **Check the vegetables and add brine, if necessary.** If enough water was released naturally to completely cover the vegetables, they can be fermented as-is. If there isn't enough brine, create a brine solution and add enough of it to the vegetables to completely submerge them. A simple brine can be made by adding 2 teaspoons of salt to 4 cups of water.

7. **OPTIONAL: Now's the time to add starter culture if you're going to add it.** Whey, kefir grains and liquid from previous fermentations are all good starter cultures.

8. **Get rid of any air pockets in the vegetables in the container.** Press the vegetables down to remove air hidden within the vegetables. A butter knife can be run around the edges of jar to get rid of visible air bubbles. If air pockets are left in the jar, this will create areas in which harmful bacteria can grow. Loosely-packed vegetables will have less air pockets than tightly packed vegetables.

9. **Press the vegetables down below the surface of the brine.** You don't want to leave any of the vegetables you're fermenting floating at the top of the brine. Vegetables exposed to the air are more likely to discolor and are more prone to growing mold. Keeping the vegetables submerged below the surface of the brine ensures they ferment in an anaerobic environment.

10. **Place a weight in the container to keep the vegetables submerged below the surface of the brine.** Smooth stones, glass plates and even folded up cabbage leaves can all be used as weights. I've also seen people use plastic bags filled with river rocks, but they seem to take up a lot of space.

11. **Add brine to the container until it's over the top of the weight.** Leave 1" to 2" of headspace at the top of the jar. This will leave a bit of airspace into which carbon dioxide can escape as it forms. Avoid leaving too much airspace because there will be too much oxygen trapped in the container with the food.

12. **Place a lid on the container and screw it down tightly.** If it's an airlock lid, follow the instructions that came with the fermenting vessel to properly seal the lid. Airtight lids are usually just screwed down tight.

13. **Store the jar in a dark area where the ambient temperature is as close to 72° F as possible.** The amount of time the jar is left to ferment depends on the vegetable being

fermented. If you're using an airtight fermenting vessel, be sure to open it periodically to release any pressure that's built up inside the jar. Airlock vessels off-gas on their own.

14. **Once the vegetables have fermented to your liking, it's time to store them.** Jars are one of the most common storage containers for fermented foods. Some people use mason jars to ferment the foods in, so all these people have to do is move the container from the warm location it was fermenting in to a cool location where fermentation is slowed to a crawl. If fermenting was done in a crock or another large container, you'll have to transfer the food to a jar before storing it.

It sounds like a lot the first time you read through it, but each step is fairly easy. The steps remain mostly the same no matter what vegetable you ferment, so once you learn the steps, you'll be good to go.

You can ferment most vegetables using this method, with only a handful of changes. The most common changes are in the processing of the vegetables and whether or not starter culture is required. There's also a significant amount of variation in fermenting times.

The key is to make sure your brine has the right amount of salt and to minimize exposure to oxygen during fermentation. For this reason, I prefer airlock containers to airtight containers because airlock containers don't have to be opened to allow them to off-gas. Airtight containers will work—as evidenced by the tens of thousands of people who use them to ferment foods daily—but they come with the added risk of exposing your fermenting vegetables to oxygen every time they're opened to release pressure.

Fermenting Vessels

One of the first decisions you're going to have to make when you decide to start making your own fermented foods is what sort of container or vessel you're going to ferment food in. There are a number of container types that can be used for fermenting vegetables. Fermenting requires an anaerobic environment, so the key is to make sure the container you're using is able to be sealed to keep outside air from getting in.

We've already discussed the two basic types of containers. Just to recap, *airtight containers* keep air from entering or leaving the container. Once they're sealed, air doesn't get in or out until the container is opened again. Airlock containers have a one-way seal. Air is prevented from entering the container, but is able to escape the container if pressure starts to build up. Airlock containers are relatively new to the world of fermenting but are beneficial in that they prevent pressure from building up and don't require the container be opened to off-gas. The food inside an airlock container is exposed to less air during the fermentation process.

You may see fermenting recipes that call for placing a cloth lid or a coffee filter over the container and using it as a cover instead of using an actual lid. It's much safer to use an airlock container to allow gases to escape than it is to use a breathable lid. Do so at your own risk.

The following container types are some of the most common fermenting vessels in use today.

Mason Jars

Mason jars are probably the most ubiquitous fermenting vessel. They're the go-to fermenting vessel for fermenters everywhere, mainly because they're inexpensive and they come in a wide variety of sizes.

They're also easy to use. All you have to do is put the food and the brine in the jar and screw the lid down tight.

Mason jars have the added benefit of being a good storage vessel once fermenting is complete. Simply move the Mason jar from the fermenting area to cold storage when fermenting is complete.

Since Mason jars are airtight, they require periodic burping. Carbon dioxide isn't able to escape as it builds up. It has to be released periodically by opening the container, which allows oxygen to get in. Another downside is the metal bands and lids may react to the acids created during fermentation.

Since mason jars aren't dedicated fermenting vessels, they don't come with a weighting system. This is only a minor irritation, since any non-reactive material can be used as a weight, but it can be a hassle to find a weight that's the right size.

Spend enough time around the world of fermenting and you'll likely come across people making the argument Mason jar ferments aren't safe. The argument is Mason jars don't seal as well as other containers, so air and oxygen is able to get inside the jars. This makes Mason jar ferments more prone to molding and the beneficial bacterial cultures found in foods fermented in Mason jars may not be as robust as those fermented in airlock containers.

While I won't argue that Mason jars do tend to let more air in than airlock containers, the specialty containers being recommended for fermenting these days have only been around a short period of time. Mason jars and similar fermenting containers have been in use for hundreds of years and some cultures ferment food in open vats. As long as the food is submerged in brine, it is fermenting in an anaerobic environment.

Airlock containers—or airlock lids—are recommended, but aren't an absolute requirement for fermenting vegetables. If all you have on hand are Mason jars, you can successfully ferment vegetables in them. Just take extra precautions to ensure the vegetables stay below the surface of the brine.

Mason Jars with Homemade Airlock Lids

Good airlock lids that are already built can be a bit on the expensive side, with the more expensive models costing $20 to $30 per lid. Airlock lids can be made for mason jars for a fraction of the price.

Here's a quick tutorial on how to make your own airlock lid:

1. **Purchase an airlock from your local beer brewing hobby store.** Bubble airlocks are the most common type and will usually run you a couple dollars.

2. **Purchase a 3/8" rubber grommet from your local hardware store.**
3. **Drill a 3/8" hole in the lid of the Mason jar.** Sand down the edges of the lid until there aren't any sharp burrs.
4. **Insert the grommet into the hole.** This will be difficult to do. Don't open the hole up more because you want a tight seal between the grommet and the lid. A butter knife works well to help maneuver the grommet into place.
5. **Next, insert the airlock into the grommet.** The airlock should fit snugly into the grommet. If the seal isn't tight, you can use a hot glue gun to cover up any gaps.

You're now the proud owner of an effective airlock fermenting vessel for somewhere in the range of $2.00 to $4.00.

Commercial Airlock Lids

There are a number of airlock fermenting containers claiming to feature the latest and greatest in airlock technology. The Pickl-Pro and the Fermenta Cap are popular choices that will get the job done, but tend to be a bit on the expensive side.

The upside to purchasing a lid instead of making your own is you don't have the hassle of trying to get the grommet to fit into the lid and the airlock to fit into the grommet. Commercial lids are guaranteed to be made from nonreactive materials, so you don't have to worry about the acids in your fermenting foods setting off a chemical reaction.

Fermenting Crocks

Jars with airlock lids come in many sizes, but it's tough to beat a fermenting crock when it comes to fermenting large batches of food. Fermenting crocks are large containers designed specifically for fermenting. They have lids that rest in a water gutter that is filled with water to create an airlock. Air isn't able to get into the container, but carbon dioxide will force its way out through the water when pressure gets too great.

Another added benefit of fermenting crocks is the fact that most crocks come with their own weighting system. The weights fit snugly into the crock and don't leave any room for food to float up around the sides.

The downside to fermenting crocks is the cost. A good fermenting crock can run a couple hundred bucks. Smaller crocks are available for around a hundred, but you generally get what you pay for. If you're planning on fermenting large batches of food, a fermenting crock will be a worthwhile investment that pays dividends over time.

Weighting Systems

Unless you buy a full fermenting kit that comes with a weighting system, you're going to have to come up with a weighting system of your own to prevent buoyant foods from floating to the top of the container and getting exposed to open air. Light vegetables that are cultured in brine have a tendency to float to the top of the brine within a couple days, so it's important they're weighted down. If they're left exposed to the open air, they can form mold and start to deteriorate.

Any weighting system you choose should have the following features:

- **It should be heavy enough to keep the vegetables below the surface of the brine and won't float to the top itself.**
- **It should fit snugly inside the container and leave no room for the vegetables to float up around the edges of the weight.**
- **The lid can be placed on the container with the weighting system in place.**
- **The weight should be made of a nonreactive material that won't chemically react to the acids created during fermentation.**
- **The weight should be smooth.** Don't use wood weights or weights made from porous stones because the pores can harbor harmful bacteria.

Glass and ceramic weights are popular, as are smooth stones. Metal weights see some use, but they have to be made of a nonreactive material. I've also heard of people using heavy rubber or plastic weights, but I'd be leery of chemicals leeching out of these weights into the fermented foods.

Salt

Salt is often added to water to create the brine used for fermentation. The addition of salt isn't an absolute necessity to ensure fermentation occurs, but it's important to helping ensure the safety of the food being fermented.

Adding salt to fermenting vegetables helps the fermentation process in a number of ways:

- **Salt pulls moisture out of the vegetables.** This allows you to create at least some brine using the natural water found in the vegetables.
- **Harmful bacteria have trouble growing when salt is present.**
- **Beneficial bacteria are able to easily grow in a salty environment.**
- **Salt keeps the vegetables crisp as they ferment.**

When it comes to salt in fermenting foods, you can have too much of a good thing. Salt slows down fermentation, which is a good thing to a certain extent. It prevents fermentation from accelerating at a rapid pace and makes it easier to control the entire process from beginning to end. The problem with salt is the more you add, the less biodiverse your end product becomes. Add too much salt and fermentation grinds to a halt. You're left with salty food that only has a small amount of beneficial bacteria.

At the low end, you can add 1 tablespoon of salt to each quart of water. This creates a more biodiverse ferment, but increases the risk of the fermented vegetables going bad. On the other end, you can add up to 4 tablespoons of salt to each quart of water to create salty brine that slows fermentation to a crawl. 2 to 3 tablespoons of salt per quart is the sweet spot for most vegetables. Bad bacteria are unlikely to grow in brine with this much salt. Fermentation still occurs at a decent clip and there will be plenty of healthy bacteria in the final product.

Sea salt and pickling salt are the two best types of salt to use for fermenting. Make sure you purchase unrefined salt with no additives. Anti-caking agents are especially harmful and can cause problems with fermentation. Steer clear of iodized table salt because it can slow or even stop the growth of beneficial flora.

Water

While you could probably get away with using tap water in a pinch, filtered water is the best type of water to use for fermenting purposes. Filtered water is best because tap water contains additives like chlorine and fluoride that can block the growth of beneficial bacteria.

Filtering your own water is an option, but be aware only the most expensive filtration systems on the market are capable of filtering out fluoride. Reverse osmosis and activated alumina deflouridation filters are capable of filtering out fluoride but are expensive to own and operate.

A better option may be buying and using bottled or filtered water that doesn't contain fluoride. Here are some of the more common bottled water brands that don't have any fluoride:

- **Alhambra.**
- **Aquafina.**
- **Aqua Pure.**
- **Arrowhead.**
- **Calistoga.**
- **Crystal Geyser.**
- **Dannon.**
- **Dasoni.**
- **Evian.**
- **Great Value.**
- **Naya.**
- **Perrier.**
- **Safeway.**

Keep in mind this isn't an all-inclusive list. There are a number of other companies that sell bottled water without fluoride. These are just some of the more popular water brands found in stores nationwide.

Starter Cultures

Starter cultures are bacterial cultures that are added to vegetables to jump-start the fermentation process. These cultures aren't always absolutely necessary, but they do help speed fermentation up.

The skins of vegetables often have all the bacterial cultures needed to get fermentation started. Many vegetables will ferment just fine without added starter cultures, albeit at a slower pace as it takes some time for the natural bacteria to really take off. Vegetables that are peeled before fermenting will need starter culture added to them to get them started in the right direction.

While the use of starter cultures isn't usually a necessity, it aids fermentation by providing a helping hand to the beneficial bacteria already present on the vegetables. Adding cultures also allows you more control over the type of cultures you end up with in the finished product. You can never be completely sure of what the final product is going to taste like, but adding starter cultures gives you at least an idea of what you're going to get. When you don't add starter cultures, the taste, texture and culturing can vary widely from batch to batch.

The following starter cultures are all common cultures that are added to fermented vegetables to give them a gentle push in the right direction.

Dried Cultures

Dried cultures are cultures that have been preserved via freeze-drying. They come in packets that are stirred into the brine. These packets give consistent results because they have specific cultures in them. You get nothing more and nothing less. They're tailor-made to be used with salt to create crunchy fermented vegetables that are less likely to grow mold during storage.

Kefir Grains

You can use either milk kefir grains or water kefir grains to ferment vegetables. Simply add a teaspoon or two of the grains to the fermenting vessel before you set it out to ferment. Don't use grains that you want to use again to make kefir, as using them to ferment vegetables will usually mean the end of their useful life as a kefir grain. Both water and milk kefir grains should only be used one time to ferment vegetables and then will need to be consumed or discarded.

Brine from a Previous Ferment

Brine from a previous ferment can be used to jumpstart a new ferment. A few tablespoons of brine are all that's needed to get your new ferment off to a good start. Be aware that the probiotic cultures in a ferment will change over time due to environmental factors beyond your control.

While brine from a previous ferment is an effective starter culture, you never know exactly what you're going to end up with as far as bacterial flora and flavor goes. It'll usually be close to what the previous ferment was like, but there are no guarantees.

Whey

Whey is a cultured milk product made by straining yogurt, kefir or buttermilk. It's dairy-based, so it isn't a good choice for those who can't handle dairy products. Vegetables fermented with whey have a different flavor than those fermented with other types of starter cultures. They don't taste bad, but they do taste different.

If you want to keep your vegetables crunchy, it's important to make sure you add salt to the recipe. Without salt to slow the fermentation process, whey will quickly ferment vegetables into a mushy mass that's tough to eat.

Here's a quick step-by-step tutorial that can be followed to make your own probiotic whey from yogurt, kefir or buttermilk:

1. **Lay a large piece of cheesecloth or a dishtowel out on the counter.**
2. **Pour the cultured yogurt, kefir or buttermilk into the center of the cloth.**
3. **Fold the corners of the piece of cloth up to create a cloth "bag" that holds the milk product.**
4. **Tie the top of the "bag" shut with a piece of string.** Leave a long enough tag end so the bag can be hung from the string.
5. **Hang the "bag" so it is suspended over a bowl into which any liquid that drains through the cloth will land in the bowl.** The bowl should be placed below the lowest point of the bottom of the bag.

6. **Let the bag hang overnight.** The whey will slowly drip through the cloth and will collect in the bowl.

The clear liquid that drains into the bowl is whey. It will last for months if stored in an airtight container in the fridge. Don't throw out the cheese in the bag. It can be used in a manner similar to how you'd use cream cheese.

Make sure the milk product you strain is probiotic. If you use uncultured milk products, the resultant whey won't have the probiotic cultures needed to get fermented foods off to a good start. Look for something on the label that indicates the product has live and active cultures.

When Are Vegetables Done Fermenting?

Fermenting is a fluid process that's dependent on a number of environmental factors, so it's tough to pinpoint exactly when vegetables are ready to be moved into cold storage. What I tell people is the vegetables are done fermenting when you feel like they're done. There is no perfect time to move vegetables into storage.

As vegetables ferment, they take on a sour smell and flavor. Some people like their vegetables more on the tart side, while others prefer just a bit of a tang to them. The longer you let the vegetables ferment, the more robust the bacterial composition will become. If you want tart vegetables packed full of probiotic bacteria, it's best to let vegetables ferment for a longer period of time. Those who want a slightly tangy vegetable that's still nice and crisp should move their vegetables into storage after only a few days of fermenting.

From a technical standpoint, vegetables never stop fermenting unless they're boiled or frozen. Heating the vegetables to extreme temperatures will kill the lactobacteria responsible for fermenting food and fermentation will grind to a halt. Freezing the vegetables will stall out fermenting by deactivating the bacteria.

The following environmental conditions have to be factored in when considering the length of time to ferment vegetables:

- **The temperature.** The perfect temperature to ferment most vegetables at is 72° F, but anything between 68° F and 75° F is considered ideal.

Vegetables will ferment slower at cooler temperatures and the fermentation process will accelerate at higher temperatures. Vegetables should not be fermented at temperatures greater than 85° F.

- **The amount of salt added to the brine.** Salt slows down fermentation. Too much salt will kill off the beneficial bacteria and fermentation won't take place.
- **Starter cultures.** If starter culture was added, vegetables will ferment faster than when no starter culture is used. When no starter culture is added, vegetables will get off to a slow start. Once fermentation gets in full swing, it can accelerate rapidly, so always watch your vegetables closely.
- **The exposed area of the vegetables being fermented.** Finely-chopped or shredded vegetables have more area exposed to the brine, so they'll ferment at a faster rate than vegetables cut into large chunks.
- **The type of vegetable being fermented.** Some vegetables—cabbage, for example—are naturally high in probiotic bacteria. These vegetables will ferment faster than vegetables that don't contain a lot of natural bacteria. Vegetables with the peel left on will ferment faster because much of the natural bacteria in vegetables resides on the peel.

There are a number of other factors that have a minor effect on fermentation times like humidity and the type and amount of bacteria there are floating around the room. Because of the numerous factors, both known and unknown, that effect fermenting times, it's impossible to know exactly when fermenting is complete.

It helps to think of the fermenting process as an art form, as opposed to it being a recipe with strict time guidelines. Like good art, it's done when it's ready.

There are a handful of indicators you can use to tell when it's approaching time to move your fermented vegetables to a cooler location:

- **There are fewer bubbles rising up through the container.** When fermenting is in full swing, small bubbles of carbon dioxide will start to rise to the surface of the brine. This will look similar to what you see when you pour a soda and see the carbonation bubbles, but usually on a smaller scale. Some ferments bubble much more vigorously than others, so don't worry if you don't see a lot of bubble action. The bubbling is usually one of the first signs fermentation is occurring. Waiting until it slows ensures a decent amount of fermentation has taken place and there are ample amounts of beneficial bacteria in the container.
- **The vegetables smell sour.** A sour smell is a sure sign vegetables are fermenting. The first few times you ferment vegetables, you'll probably find yourself wondering whether the

vegetables are starting to go bad or are fermenting. Once you've done it for a while, you'll become accustomed to the distinctly sour smell of properly fermented vegetables. It helps to have someone who knows how to ferment foods around to provide guidance the first few times you ferment vegetables.

- **The vegetables have a tangy taste.** The taste of fermented vegetables is unmistakable. They will have a tangy taste with a bit of a bite to it.

It's important to remember that fermentation doesn't actually stop when vegetables are moved into cold storage. The process slows down, but the vegetables will continue to slowly ferment. If you plan on storing them for an extended period of time, it's best to move vegetables to cold storage before they reach the point where you'd like to eat them.

How to Store Fermented Vegetables

Fermented vegetables need to be stored in a cool, dark place. Some people keep them in a cool pantry or root cellar, while others prefer to store them in the fridge. The fridge is generally cooler than a pantry or a root cellar, so fermented vegetables will last longer when they're stored there. The cooler the area the vegetables are stored in, the more fermentation will slow down.

Vegetables that are fermented in mason jars can be left in the jars when they're moved to storage. If you're using airlock containers, you can take off the airlock lids and replace them with regular airtight lids before placing them in storage. Since fermentation will slow to a crawl, pressure isn't much of a concern unless the jars are stored for long periods of time. Make sure the lids you use are BPA-free and are made of a non-reactive material.

Vegetables that have been fermented in larger containers like fermenting crocks can be moved to airtight jars for storage. Don't attempt to store the vegetables in the crock. Once the water around the lid dries, the food inside will be exposed to open air and the food can go bad.

Make sure the vegetables stay submerged in brine when you pack them away for storage. Foods that are left exposed are more prone to mold and are much more likely to go bad.

Properly fermented vegetables don't go bad inasmuch as they simply get soft and degrade to the point where they're no longer palatable. Most people prefer crisp vegetables and don't want to eat soft, squishy vegetables that are strongly acidic. Vegetables left to ferment for too long will eventually turn into a soft mush.

How to Tell When Fermented Vegetables Have Gone Bad

It doesn't happen often, but fermented vegetables can occasionally go bad. Eating spoiled foods can make you very ill and death is a possibility. Use common sense and never eat food you suspect has gone bad. The truth is illness from fermented foods is relatively rare, but you should still take precautions to make sure you don't end up eating bad foods.

Here are some signs to look for that may indicate food has gone bad:

- **It smells rotten.** Don't confuse this with the tangy, sour smell that is natural to fermented foods. If your food has a rotten scent to it, don't eat it.
- **Mold.** Food that's exposed to too much oxygen or is allowed to float to the surface of the brine can start to grow mold. Some books say it's an acceptable practice to get rid of the moldy food and the food beneath it should be fine. While this may be the case, mold grows by sending out invisible feelers that attach to other pieces of food. The food below the visibly moldy pieces could be infected with mold as well—and you'll never know it. For this reason, it's best to toss out moldy containers of food.
- **Brown spots in the food.** Brown spots or other discolored spots in the food may indicate the

food has started to turn. Toss out any vegetables that develop dark spots or brown spots.

- **Slimy brine or vegetables.** Slime is indicative of food that's starting to turn. Get rid of food that has a slimy texture or brine that feels viscous.
- **Food has a rotten taste.** Taste is your last line of defense. Don't eat food that's showing any of the other signs of going bad. If the fermented vegetables don't taste right when you put them in your mouth, spit them out and wash out your mouth.

Use common sense when it comes to food you think may be spoiled. Food that's showing any of the above signs should be discarded. It's better to get rid of a batch of food than it is to eat it and hope for the best. Eating bad food can make you violently ill, so it's imperative you remain diligent.

Fermented Vegetable Recipes

Here it is. The chapter you've been waiting for—the recipes. All of the recipes in this chapter use lacto-fermentation to ferment vegetables. The best part is they're all simple recipes that only require a minimal amount of preparation.

Asparagus

I've always been a big fan of asparagus. There's just something about those succulent green spears I can't resist. Cultured asparagus takes asparagus to the next level. It's a crisp, tangy treat that goes great on salads, as a side dish or as a simple and healthy snack.

Selection:

Choose freshly-picked asparagus shoots that are 6" to 8" long. Asparagus starts to degrade rapidly once it's harvested, so process your asparagus quickly. Slender shoots are better than thicker shoots because the thicker shoots tend to be fibrous.

Ingredients:

3 to 4 pounds of asparagus.

1 lemon.

4 garlic cloves.

2 tablespoons sea salt.

Filtered water.

Starter Culture:

Yes. Use ¼ cup of whey, a few tablespoons of liquid from a previous ferment or a packet of vegetable starter culture.

Instructions:

1. Wash the asparagus.
2. Cut off the bottom inch or two of the stalk.

3. Place the asparagus into the fermenting vessel(s). Stand it up so it fills the container to within a few inches of the top. If you're using smaller jars, the asparagus can be cut into 3" to 4" pieces. Fill the jar with the smaller pieces.
4. Wash and slice the lemon.
5. Peel the garlic cloves.
6. Add 1 lemon slice and 1 to 2 garlic cloves to each of the containers.
7. Create brine by mixing 2 tablespoons of sea salt with 4 cups of water.
8. Fill the vessel(s) with brine.
9. Place the weight in the vessel(s) and press it down. The weight should be submerged beneath the surface of the brine. Add more brine if necessary. Leave a 1" to 2" headspace at the top of each container.
10. Seal the container(s). The method used to seal the container varies from container to container, so check the directions that came with your container.
11. Place the vessel(s) in a dark area of your house with an ambient temperature of around 72° F. Let the asparagus ferment until it's fermented to your liking. Don't forget to burp airtight containers once a day.

Fermenting time:

Asparagus can be left to ferment for up to a week. Start checking it after 4 days to see if it has fermented to your preference.

Fermented Shredded Beets

We've been blessed the past few years with good harvests of beets. So good, in fact, I found myself running out of ideas for what to do with them. For some reason, I never thought about fermenting them until recently. I'm glad I did, because this recipe has allowed us to preserve our beet harvest and has quickly become a family favorite. Well, at least for the older members of the family. The kids still grumble when they see me break out the jars of beets.

This recipe comes with a warning.

If you're using an airtight container, make sure you off-gas it once a day while it's fermenting. I forgot to do this once and bright red beet juice sprayed all over my kitchen when I opened the container. Rest assured that after hours of scrubbing everything the juice came in contact with (and throwing away my favorite curtains), I am extremely cautious when it comes to opening fermented beet containers.

Selection:

Select beets that are firm to the touch and are in prime condition for eating.

Ingredients:

8 to 10 beets.

3 tablespoons sea salt.

Filtered water.

Starter Culture:

Starter culture can be added to this recipe to help get it off to a good start. Use ¼ cup of whey, a packet of starter culture or a couple tablespoons of liquid from a previous ferment.

Instructions:

1. Wash the beets.
2. Shred the beets.
3. Place the beets in a bowl and mix the sea salt into the beets.
4. Cover the bowl and let it sit for a couple hours.
5. Move the beets into the fermenting vessel(s).
6. If the beets didn't release enough natural moisture to create brine, add filtered water until the beets are covered.
7. Add the starter culture to the fermenting vessel, if you plan on using it.
8. Place the weight in the container and press it down. The weight should be submerged beneath the surface of the brine. Add more brine if necessary. Leave a 1" to 2" headspace at the top of the container.
9. Seal the container. The method used to seal the container varies from container to container, so check the directions that came with your container.
10. Place the container in a dark area of your house with an ambient temperature of around 72° F. Let the beets ferment until they have fermented to your liking. Don't forget to burp airtight containers once a day.

Fermenting time:

The beets should be left to ferment for 2 to 3 days. Move them to cold storage once fermenting is complete.

Beet Kvass

Beet kvass is a tradition Ukrainian fermented beverage. The original kvass was made by fermenting stale bread and is a staple beverage across Russia. This kvass thankfully doesn't require fermenting bread. Instead, it uses beets to create a fermented beverage that tastes a lot better than you might think it would.

A half-gallon jar works best for this recipe.

Selection:

Choose fully-formed beets that are prime for eating.

Ingredients:

5 beets.

1 tablespoon sea salt.

Filtered water.

Starter Culture:

Yes. Use ¼ cup of whey or 3 tablespoons of juice from a previous ferment.

Instructions:

1. Wash the beets and remove the peels.
2. Chop the beets into small pieces.
3. Place the beets in the bottom of the fermenting vessel.
4. Add the sea salt and the starter culture to the vessel.
5. Fill the jar to within 2" of the top with filtered water.

6. Place the lid on the container and let it ferment at room temperature.

Fermenting time:

Beet kvass should be allowed to ferment for 2 to 3 days at room temperature before it's moved to the fridge.

Beet Kanji

Kanji is a traditional Indian beverage that's similar to beet kvass, but has added vegetables and spices. This beverage has strong antioxidant properties because of the beets, the ginger and the probiotic bacteria. It has a refreshing tangy taste with a spicy aftertaste. Drinking a cup of kanji leaves you feeling healthy and rejuvenated.

Don't throw out the beets and carrots. They can be eaten as a snack or added to salads to give them a probiotic boost.

Selection:

Choose fully-formed beets that are prime for eating. Use medium carrots that are still tender.

Ingredients:

2 beets.

1 medium carrot.

1 teaspoon fresh ginger root, grated.

3 teaspoons mustard powder.

1 teaspoon red pepper flakes.

1 tablespoon salt.

Filtered water.

Starter Culture:

Starter culture generally isn't added to this recipe.

Instructions:

1. Wash the beets and remove the peels.
2. Chop the beets into small pieces.

3. Wash and peel the carrot.
4. Slice the carrot into thin slices.
5. Add all of the ingredients to the fermenting vessel. Stir in the ginger root, mustard powder, pepper flakes and the salt.
6. Fill the jar to within 1" of the top with filtered water.
7. Seal the container and let it ferment at room temperature. Burp the container once a day.

Fermenting time:

Beet kanji should be allowed to ferment for up to 5 days at room temperature before it's moved to the fridge. You'll know it's ready once the beets have bled most of their color into the water.

Brussels Sprouts

Brussels sprouts are a close relative of cabbage. Seeing as cabbage is one of the most-widely fermented vegetables, it stands to reason Brussels sprouts would be a good candidate for fermenting as well. The best part about this recipe is it eliminates much of the bitterness from the Brussels sprouts. Kids may be more willing to eat fermented sprouts than they are regular cooked sprouts.

Selection:

Select Brussels sprouts that are in prime condition for eating. They should have firm heads and should be green and unwilted.

Ingredients:

1 to 2 pounds of Brussels sprouts.

2 green onions.

2 teaspoons red pepper flakes.

2 tablespoons sea salt.

Filtered water.

Starter Culture:

Yes. Use ¼ cup of whey or a packet of vegetables starter culture with this recipe.

Instructions:

1. Wash the Brussels sprouts and green onions.
2. Cut the Brussels sprouts in half.
3. Chop up the green onions.

4. Place the onions and Brussels sprouts in the fermenting vessel.
5. Add the red pepper flakes to the container.
6. Create brine by mixing 2 tablespoons of sea salt with 4 cups of water.
7. Fill the vessel with brine.
8. Place the weight in the vessel and press it down. The weight should be submerged beneath the surface of the brine. Add more brine if necessary. Leave a 1" to 2" headspace at the top of the container.
9. Seal the container. The method used to seal the container varies from container to container, so check the directions that came with your container.
10. Place the vessel in a dark area of your house with an ambient temperature of around 72° F. Let the Brussels sprouts ferment until they've fermented to your liking. Don't forget to burp airtight containers once a day.

Fermenting time:

Let Brussels sprouts ferment for 7 to 10 days. Start checking them after 5 days and move them to cold storage once they've fermented to your liking.

Cultured Cucumber Salad

This is a great cultured salad that pairs well with meals and works well as an afternoon snack. It'll last a month or two in the fridge, but it's unlikely you'll have to worry about it lasting that long.

Selection:

Choose fresh vegetables that are in prime eating condition.

Ingredients:

4 medium cucumbers.

1 medium onion.

1 green bell pepper.

1 red bell pepper.

1 teaspoon red pepper flakes.

1 teaspoon celery flakes.

2 tablespoons sea salt.

Filtered water.

Starter Culture:

Yes. Use ¼ cup of whey, a packet of vegetable starter culture or a few tablespoons of liquid from a previous ferment.

Instructions:

1. Wash and peel the cucumbers.
2. Slice them into thin slices.
3. Wash the onion and slice it.

4. Wash the bell peppers. Cut them in half and remove the seeds and the cores.
5. Add the cucumbers, red onions and bell peppers to the fermenting vessel.
6. Create brine by combining 4 cups of water with 2 tablespoons of sea salt.
7. Fill the vessel with brine. Leave room for the weight. Get rid of any air bubbles that form in the container.
8. Add the starter culture and the rest of the ingredients.
9. Place the weight into the vessel and press it down. The weight should be below the surface of the brine. Add more brine, if necessary. Leave 1" of headspace.
10. Place the lid on the container and seal it.
11. Let the container ferment in an area with an ambient temperature as close to 72° F as you can get. Burp the container once a day.

Fermenting time:

Cultured cucumber salad should be fermented for 3 to 5 days. Start checking it after the 3rd day and move it to cold storage when it's ready.

Curtido

Curtido is a cultured Mexican and Central American dish that's reminiscent of sauerkraut, but has more kick to it. My first experience with it was having it served over pupusas, which are thick tortillas with cheese, meat and beans cooked into them. It can be added to burritos, tacos and enchiladas and I've even used it as a condiment on hot dogs. It can also be served as a side dish accompanying most Mexican foods.

Selection:

Use freshly harvested heads of cabbage. Do not use cabbage that has started to wilt or has browning leaf ends. Select mature carrots that are firm to the touch.

Ingredients:

2 heads of cabbage.

5 carrots.

2 onions.

1 tablespoon crushed red pepper.

1 tablespoon dried oregano.

1 teaspoon cumin.

2 tablespoons sea salt.

Starter Culture:

Starter culture can be used with this recipe. Add ¼ to ½ cup fresh whey to the recipe to give it a probiotic boost.

Instructions:

1. Wash the cabbage. Core it and shred it.
2. Place the shredded cabbage in a bowl. As you finish each head of cabbage, sprinkle sea salt on top and pound it with a kraut hammer.
3. Wash the carrots and shred them. Add the carrots to the bowl.
4. Peel the onions and dice them.
5. Add all of the ingredients to a bowl and mash them using a kraut hammer.
6. Place the curtido into the fermenting vessel(s). Pack it in as tightly as you can get it. Remove any visible air bubbles.
7. Press the weight down into the vessel(s). Place the lid on the container(s) and let them sit overnight.
8. Press the weight down again. The natural juices released by the cabbage should be over the top of the weight and the curtido should be held beneath the surface of the brine by the weight. Add more brine if necessary. Leave a 1" to 2" headspace at the top of the container.
9. Seal the container. The method used to seal the container varies from container to container, so check the directions that came with your container.
10. Place the container in a dark area of your house with an ambient temperature of around 72° F. Let the curtido ferment until it has fermented to your liking. Don't forget to burp airtight containers every couple of days.

Fermenting time:

It can take up to a month for curtido to properly ferment. Check it once every 2 to 3 days and move it to cold storage once it's fermented to your preference.

Curried Cauliflower

Cauliflower on its own is a bland vegetable with little flavor. Add curry and a handful of other spices to it and ferment it and you end up with a tasty dish that's a bit on the spicy side, but not overpowering. This dish is best eaten as a snack or served as a side dish.

Selection:

Use fresh cauliflower with tightly-packed heads.

Ingredients:

2 heads of cauliflower.

5 garlic cloves.

3 tablespoons curry powder.

1 teaspoon turmeric.

Cayenne pepper, to taste.

2 tablespoons sea salt.

Filtered water.

Starter Culture:

Starter culture can be used with this recipe. Add ¼ to ½ cup fresh whey or a packet of vegetable starter culture to get it off to a good start.

Instructions:

1. Wash the cauliflower heads and break them up into small florets.
2. Peel the garlic cloves and chop them into chunks.

3. Place the cauliflower and spices into the fermenting vessel.
4. Create brine by mixing 4 cups of filtered water with 2 tablespoons of sea salt.
5. Fill the vessel with brine. Get rid of any air bubbles that form.
6. Press the weight down into the vessel. The brine should be over the top of the weight. Add more brine if necessary. Leave a 1" to 2" headspace at the top of the container.
7. Seal the container. The method used to seal the container varies from container to container, so check the directions that came with your container.
8. Place the container in a dark area of your house with an ambient temperature of around 72° F. Let the cauliflower ferment until it has fermented to your liking. Don't forget to burp airtight containers every couple of days.

Fermenting time:

Curried cauliflower takes 2 to 3 days to ferment.

Dilly Carrots

Dilly carrots are one of my favorite snacks. I almost always have a jar of these crunchy pickled carrots in my fridge—and I usually have a jar or two in the pantry fermenting as well. In addition to being great snacks, they can also be used to add probiotic goodness to all sorts of salads.

Selection:

Choose small to medium carrots that have recently been harvested.

Ingredients:

6 to 8 small to medium carrots.

3 garlic cloves.

2 tablespoons fresh dill leaves.

1 tablespoon dill seeds.

3 tablespoons sea salt.

4 cups filtered water.

Starter Culture:

Yes. Add ¼ cup of whey, 1 packet of dried cultures or 2 to 3 tablespoons of liquid from a previous ferment to this recipe.

Instructions:

1. Wash the carrots. Peel them and cut them into carrot sticks. Alternatively, smaller carrots can be peeled and cut down to where they just fit into the fermenting vessel.

2. Peel the garlic and chop it into small pieces.
3. Place the carrots and the garlic into the fermenting vessel.
4. Add the dill leaves and the dill seeds to the container.
5. Mix the sea salt and the water together.
6. Fill the container with brine until the brine is just over the top of the carrots. Remove any air bubbles that form.
7. Add the starter culture to the container.
8. Place the weight in the container. Press the weight down into the container. Leave a 1" to 2" headspace at the top of the container.
9. Seal the container. The method used to seal the container varies from container to container, so check the directions that came with your container.
10. Place the container in a dark area of your house with an ambient temperature of around 72° F and let it ferment until the dilly carrots are fermented to your liking.

Fermenting time:

Let the dilly carrots ferment for 5 to 7 days. Check them after 5 days and then check them once a day after that. Airtight jars will need to be burped once a day.

Ginger Lemon Carrots

These carrots are more a condiment than they are a side dish. They taste great when served over fish or pork or even when added to a lunchmeat sandwich.They can also be added to salad or coleslaw to give it a probiotic boost.

Selection:

Select medium carrots that do not have any fibrous portions.

Ingredients:

8 medium carrots.

3 tablespoons fresh shredded ginger.

2 teaspoons lemon zest.

2 tablespoons sea salt.

Filtered water.

Starter Culture:

Yes. Add ¼ cup whey to this recipe to get it off to a good start.

Instructions:

1. Wash the carrots. Peel them and grate them. Use the large holes on the grater.
2. Place the carrots into the fermenting vessel.
3. Stir in the lemon zest and the shredded ginger.
4. Combine the 2 tablespoons of sea salt with 4 cups of filtered water and add water to the container until the carrots are covered. Remove any air bubbles that form.

5. Add the whey to the vessel.
6. Place the weight in the container. Press the weight down into the container. Leave a 1" to 2" headspace at the top of the container.
7. Seal the container. The method used to seal the container varies from container to container, so check the directions that came with your container.
8. Place the container in a dark area of your house with an ambient temperature of around 72° F and leave the carrots until they've fermented to your preference.

Fermenting time:

Let the ginger lemon carrots ferment for 3 to 5 days. Check them after 3 days and then check them once a day until they're ready to be moved into cold storage.

Spicy Hot Chili Sauce

Here's a fact most people don't know. Tabasco sauce is created by combining chilies with salt and letting the chilies ferment in oak barrels for as long as three years. The peppers are then mixed with vinegar. After a month or so, the solid parts of the peppers are strained away from the sauce, which is then bottled and shipped across the country.

While you aren't going to get an exact match, you can make a similar chili sauce at home—and your sauce will have the added benefit of being full of beneficial bacteria.

Selection:

Choose ripe peppers that are firm to the touch. Do not use peppers with visible damage or soft spots. The type of pepper you use will determine how hot the final product is. Habanero peppers can be used to make an extremely hot sauce, whereas your face off.

Ingredients:

5 to 6 pounds of chili peppers.

5 garlic cloves.

3 tablespoons sugar.

2 tablespoons sea salt.

Starter Culture:

Yes. Use ¼ cup of whey or a packet of vegetable starter culture.

Instructions:

1. Wash the peppers and remove the stems.

2. Peel the garlic.
3. Combine all of the ingredients in a blender or food processor and blend into a paste.
4. Place the paste into a fermenting vessel. Leave 2" of headspace in the container.
5. Add ¼ cup of whey or a packet of vegetable starter culture to the vessel.
6. Place the lid on the container and seal it.
7. Let the container ferment in an area with an ambient temperature as close to 72° F as you can get.

Fermenting time:

Let the chili sauce ferment for 5 to 7 days. Once it has finished fermenting, push the sauce through a sieve and move it to cold storage.

Cultured Dilly Beans

Dilly beans are a time-honored traditional snack in the Midwest. They've traditionally been pickled in vinegar, but this recipe switches things up a bit and ferments them. In my opinion, fermenting dilly beans makes them even better. It gives them a tangy, fizzy flavor and adds probiotic bacteria to them.

Dilly beans are a great side dish that can be paired successfully with a wide variety of meat, poultry and fish dishes. They can also be eaten as a snack anytime you want something healthy and filling.

Selection:

Use green beans that have been freshly harvested. Avoid using green beans with visible damage or beans that have started to turn brown.

Ingredients:

2 to 3 pounds of green beans.

3 garlic cloves.

2 tablespoons fresh dill leaves.

1 tablespoon dill seeds.

3 tablespoons sea salt.

4 cups filtered water.

Starter Culture:

Yes. Add ¼ cup of whey, 1 packet of dried cultures or 2 to 3 tablespoons of liquid from a previous ferment to this recipe.

Instructions:

1. Wash the green beans.
2. Break or cut off the ends of the green beans. Larger beans can be cut or broken in half to fit them in the jar.
3. Peel the garlic and chop it into small pieces.
4. Place the green beans and the garlic into the fermenting vessel.
5. Add the dill leaves and the dill seeds to the container.
6. Mix the sea salt and the water together to create brine.
7. Fill the container with brine until the brine is just over the top of the green beans. Remove any air bubbles that form.
8. Add the starter culture to the container.
9. Place the weight in the container. Press the weight down into the container. Leave a 1" to 2" headspace at the top of the container.
10. Seal the container. The method used to seal the container varies from container to container, so check the directions that came with your container.
11. Place the container in a dark area of your house with an ambient temperature of around 72° F and let it ferment until the dilly beans are fermented to your liking.

Fermenting time:

Let the dilly beans ferment for 3 to 5 days. Check them after 3 days and then check them once a day after that.

Move the dilly beans to cold storage once they've fermented to your liking.

Peppered Garlic Green Beans

I thought dilly beans were the pinnacle of flavor when it came to green beans until I tried this recipe. Peppered garlic green beans are absolutely delicious, as long as you don't mind your green beans being a little spicy.

Capsaicin is the compound in peppers responsible for the burning sensation you experience when you eat them. There is a number of health benefits associated with capsaicin. This spicy chemical compound has antioxidant qualities and is believed to boost metabolism. In addition to capsaicin, jalapeno peppers are packed with a number of other vitamins and nutrients, including vitamins A, B6 and C.

It's a good idea to wear gloves when handling the peppers. Avoid touching sensitive areas of the skin after handling the peppers.

Selection:

Use green beans that have been freshly harvested. Avoid using green beans with visible damage or beans that have started to turn brown. The cayenne peppers should be firm to the touch and have skin that's tightly stretched.

Ingredients:

1 pound of green beans.

4 garlic cloves.

2 cayenne peppers.

1 tablespoon red pepper flakes.

2 tablespoons sea salt.

4 cups filtered water.

Starter Culture:

Yes. Add ¼ cup of whey, 1 packet of dried cultures or 2 to 3 tablespoons of liquid from a previous ferment to this recipe.

Instructions:

1. Wash the green beans.
2. Break or cut off the ends of the green beans. Larger beans can be cut or broken in half to fit them in the jar.
3. Peel the garlic and chop it into small pieces.
4. Place the green beans, peppers and the garlic into the fermenting vessel.
5. Mix the sea salt and the water together to create brine.
6. Fill the container with brine until the brine is just over the top of the green beans. Remove any air bubbles that form.
7. Add the starter culture and the red pepper flakes to the container.
8. Place the weight in the container. Press the weight down into the container. Leave a 1" to 2" headspace at the top of the container.
9. Seal the container. The method used to seal the container varies from container to container, so check the directions that came with your container.
10. Place the container in a dark area of your house with an ambient temperature of around 72° F and

let it ferment until the green beans are fermented to your liking.

Fermenting time:

Let the green beans ferment for 3 to 5 days. Check them after 3 days and then check them once a day after that. Move the green beans to cold storage once they've fermented to your liking.

Jalapeno Spread

Let me begin by definitively stating this recipe isn't for everyone. If you love spicy foods, you'll love this jalapeno spread. If you aren't a fan of spicy foods, this recipe is probably one you're going to want to skip over. Add this spread to burgers or use it to spice up nachos and other Mexican food dishes. Add it to the dishes after cooking them in order to avoid killing off the probiotic bacteria.

It's always a good idea to wear gloves when handling hot peppers. Avoid touching sensitive areas of the body and make sure you wash your hands once you're done handling the peppers.

Selection:

Select jalapenos that are prime for eating. They should be firm to the touch and free of visible damage.

Ingredients:

40 jalapenos.

5 garlic cloves.

2 tablespoons sea salt.

2 tablespoons sugar.

Starter Culture:

Yes. Use ¼ cup of whey with this recipe.

Instructions:

1. Wash the peppers.

2. Slice them in half lengthwise and remove the seeds. It's a good idea to wear gloves while handling the peppers.
3. Peel the garlic.
4. Place the jalapenos and the rest of the ingredients in a blender or food processor and blend together. You can leave it chunky or blend it into a paste.
5. Place the spread into the fermenting vessel.
6. Seal the container following the manufacturer's instructions.
7. Leave the container to ferment at room temperature.

Fermenting time:

Allow jalapeno paste to ferment for a couple days and then move it to cold storage.

Lemon Kale and Cabbage

The flavors of kale and cabbage blend together wonderfully in this lemon-infused blend of salad vegetables. Add this fermented dish to salads and soups, or place a spoonful or two on top of scrambled or fried eggs.

Selection:

Choose cabbage and kale that is fresh and hasn't started to wilt.

Ingredients:

1 head of cabbage.

4 cups kale.

1 lemon.

½ of a medium onion.

4 cloves garlic.

2 tablespoons sea salt.

1 teaspoon sugar.

Filtered water.

Starter Culture:

Starter culture can be used with this recipe, but it isn't a necessity. If you decide to use starter culture, ¼ cup of whey, a few tablespoons of liquid from a previous ferment or a packet of vegetable starter culture are all good options.

Instructions:

1. Wash the vegetables.

2. Remove the tough outer leaves from the cabbage. Core the cabbage and cut it into thin slices.
3. Remove the thick stalks from the kale and break it up into smaller pieces.
4. Place the kale and the cabbage in a bowl. Add the sea salt to the bowl and stir it into the cabbage.
5. Peel the lemon. Remove as much of the pith as possible. Cut the lemon in half.
6. Peel and dice the onion.
7. Peel and mince the garlic.
8. Add the onion and the garlic to the bowl and stir it in.
9. Divide the contents of the bowl into two fermenting vessels.
10. Add half a lemon and a couple cloves of garlic to each container.
11. Create brine by adding 2 tablespoons of sea salt to 4 cups of filtered water and stirring it in. Add the sugar and stir it in as well.
12. Fill the containers with brine. Leave room for the weight.
13. Add starter culture at this time, if you plan on using it. Get rid of any air bubbles that exist in the container.
14. Press the weight down into each vessel. Leave 1" to 2" of headspace at the top of the container.
15. Seal the container. The method used to seal the container varies from container to container, so

check the directions that came with your
container.

16. Place the container in a dark area of your house
with an ambient temperature of around 72° F.
Let the kale and cabbage ferment until it has
fermented to your liking.

Fermenting time:

This recipe can take up to a week to ferment. Start
checking it after 3 days and move it to cold storage once it
has fermented to your liking.

Probiotic Ketchup

Buy ketchup at the grocery store and you're more than likely buying unhealthy ketchup full of high fructose corn syrup. The corn syrup used in commercial ketchup is more than likely made with GMO corn, as is the vinegar used to make the ketchup.

Additionally, the tomatoes are processed under high heat, which removes most of their health value. Then, "natural" flavors are added, which could be anything that is derived from a natural product. This isn't a problem for most people, but those with food allergies could have a reaction to something derived from a natural product without even realizing it.

Making your own ketchup at home is a much better alternative. Fermented ketchup is even better because it adds probiotic bacteria to your favorite condiment. This ketchup is pretty much guilt-free, so feel free to use it as you please.

Selection:

Choose ripe tomatoes that are firm to the touch, but yield under gentle pressure.

Ingredients:

12 pounds paste tomatoes.

¼ cup honey.

4 tablespoons apple cider vinegar.

1 teaspoon ground cloves.

3 teaspoons allspice.

2 tablespoons sea salt.

Starter Culture:

Yes. Use ½ cup of whey.

Instructions:

1. Wash the tomatoes and remove the stems.
2. Bring a pot of water to a boil and place the tomatoes in the boiling water until they split open. This should take less than a minute.
3. Transfer the tomatoes to an ice water bath. Once they've cooled, peel off the skins.
4. Cut the tomatoes in half and remove the seeds and gel.
5. Place the tomatoes in a blender or food processor and blend them into a puree.
6. Place the tomato puree into a pot and bring the pot to a boil. Back it off to a simmer and cook the tomatoes for 20 to 30 minutes. Pass them through a sieve to get rid of any leftover seeds or skin.
7. Add the vinegar, ground cloves and allspice to the tomato paste and stir them in.
8. Place the tomato paste into a slow cooker and cook it until it reaches the consistency you want your ketchup to have. This can take up to 12 hours.
9. Once the ketchup has reached the desired consistency, turn off the heat and let it cool.
10. Add the honey, sea salt and the whey and stir it in.
11. Place the lid on the container and seal it.

12. Let the container ferment in an area with an ambient temperature as close to 72° F as you can get. Open airtight containers once a day to allow built-up gases to escape.

Fermenting time:

Probiotic ketchup should be fermented for 3 to 4 days before being moved to cold storage.

Kimchi

Growing up I was lucky enough to be good friends with a Korean family who introduced me to kimchi at an early age. Kimchi is a traditional Korean dish made up of a number of fermented vegetables, with cabbage being front and center. I have to admit I didn't care much for kimchi the first couple times I tried it, but it's grown on me and now I love it.

Selection:

Use freshly harvested heads of cabbage. Do not use cabbage that has started to wilt or has browning leaf ends. The carrots should be medium carrots that have been freshly harvested.

Ingredients:

2 heads of cabbage.

15 cloves of garlic.

4 medium carrots.

1 daikon radish.

2 tablespoons fresh grated ginger.

1 cup chili powder.

½ cup fish sauce.

5 tablespoons sea salt.

2 teaspoons sugar.

½ teaspoon cayenne pepper.

Filtered water.

Starter Culture:

Starter culture can be added, but isn't a necessity. If you do add starter culture, ¼ cup of whey or a few tablespoons of liquid from a previous ferment will work well.

Instructions:

1. Wash the cabbage. Core it and chop it into 1" to 2" pieces.
2. Place the cabbage in a bowl. As you finish chopping each head of cabbage, sprinkle sea salt on top.
3. Place the cabbage in a large bowl. Cover the bowl and let it sit for 6 hours.
4. Add the garlic, ginger, chili powder, fish sauce, cayenne pepper and sugar to a blender and blend it into a paste.
5. Wash the carrots. Peel them and cut them into thin strips.
6. Chop the radish up into small pieces.
7. After the cabbage has sat for 6 hours, squeeze as much moisture out of it as you can.
8. Add the chili paste, carrots and the radish to the bowl and stir everything together.
9. Place the contents of the bowl into the fermenting vessels.
10. Press the weight down into each vessel. Place the lid on the containers and let them sit overnight.
11. Press the weight down again. The kimchi should be submerged in chili paste. Add more chili paste, if necessary. Leave a 1" to 2" headspace at the top of the container.

12. Seal the container. The method used to seal the container varies from container to container, so check the directions that came with your container.
13. Place the container in a dark area of your house with an ambient temperature of around 72° F. Let the kimchi ferment until it has fermented to your liking.

Fermenting time:

Kimchi is usually left to ferment for a couple days. You'll know it's ready to be moved into cold storage when you see bubbles start to form.

Kohlrabi Pickles

Most people aren't familiar with kohlrabi. I was in the same boat until I came across it at a local farmer's market last year. I'd seen these bulbous stems before in the produce section at the grocery store and passed them by, but for some reason I was feeling adventurous and bought a few. After a bit of research, I found they're a member of the cabbage family. The portion that is consumed is the bulbous portion of the plant that grows just above ground level. They taste like turnips, only milder. The leaves are also edible and make a great addition to salads.

If you're a fan of dill pickles, these kohlrabi pickles should be right up your alley. They're easy to make and have a satisfying crunch when bitten into.

Selection:

Choose blemish-free kohlrabi that fit easily into the palm of your hand. Larger kohlrabi stems tend to be tough and woody. 2" to 3" diameter stems are the best for this recipe.

Ingredients:

3 to 4 kohlrabi bulbs.

2 garlic cloves.

2 tablespoons sea salt.

2 tablespoons dill leaves.

1 tablespoon dill seeds.

Filtered water.

Starter Culture:

Yes. Use ¼ cup of whey, a packet of vegetable starter culture or a few tablespoons of liquid from a previous ferment.

Instructions:

1. Remove the leaves and stems from the kohlrabi bulbs.
2. Wash the bulbs.
3. Peel the kohlrabi and slice them into coins.
4. Peel and mince the garlic cloves.
5. Add the kohlrabi coins, garlic, dill leaves and dill seeds to the fermenting vessel.
6. Create brine by combining 4 cups of water with 2 tablespoons of sea salt.
7. Fill the vessel with brine. Leave room for the weight. Get rid of any air bubbles that form in the container.
8. Add the starter culture.
9. Place the weight into the vessel and press it down. The weight should be below the surface of the brine. Add more brine, if necessary. Leave 1" of headspace.
10. Place the lid on the container and seal it.
11. Let the container ferment in an area with an ambient temperature as close to 72° F as you can get. Burp the container once a day.

Fermenting time:

Kohlrabi should be left to ferment for up to a week. Check it once a day after the 4th day and move it to cold storage once it has fermented to your liking.

Cultured Horseradish Mustard

Seeing this recipe through to completion is going to take patience. While most recipes take a week and sauerkraut can take up to a month, this recipe can take up to 6 months to properly age. If you want to have cultured mustard to use all the time, it's going to take some serious planning ahead.

This mustard isn't for the faint of heart. The horseradish and mustard combine to punch you right in the taste buds. A little bit of this mustard goes a long way.

Selection:

Choose firm horseradish roots that have been freshly harvested.

Ingredients:

¼ cup brown mustard seeds.

¼ cup yellow mustard seeds.

2 cloves garlic.

½ medium onion.

3 tablespoons horseradish root.

3 dried chili peppers.

1 tablespoon salt.

Filtered water.

Starter Culture:

Yes. Use ¼ teaspoon of starter culture from a vegetable starter culture packet or a tablespoon of liquid from a previous ferment.

Instructions:

1. Fill the fermenting vessel with the ingredients for this recipe. If you have a large fermenting vessel, increase the ingredients across the board to fill the jar.
2. Add the starter culture.
3. Create brine by combining 4 cups of water with 1 tablespoon of sea salt.
4. Pour the brine over the top of the ingredients. Fill the vessel to the rim with brine.
5. Cover the container and let it sit overnight. The brine will be absorbed by the seeds. Fill the container with brine again in the morning.
6. Place the lid on the container and seal it.
7. Let the container ferment in an area with an ambient temperature as close to 72° F as you can get. Burp the container once a day.
8. Let the mustard ferment for 7 days. After 7 days have passed, blend the mustard into a puree using a blender or food processor.
9. Place the mustard in an airtight container in the fridge and let it age for 4 to 6 months before eating it.

Fermenting time:

The first ferment should be for 7 days. After the initial ferment, place the mustard in the fridge for 4 to 6 months to age.

Fermented Onions

Raw onions have a strong taste and aroma that not everyone can handle. Once they've been cooked, the flavor is much more mild and palatable. Fermented onions fall somewhere between raw and cooked onions. The bite that accompanies raw onions is less intense, but there's still a bit of it left. Fermented onions are a great addition to salads and are a tasty topping for hamburgers and hot dogs.

Selection:

Choose onions that are firm to the touch and undamaged.

Ingredients:

5 medium onions.

3 tablespoons sea salt.

Filtered water.

Starter Culture:

This simple recipe requires nothing more than onions and brine. Starter culture can be added, but isn't necessary.

Instructions:

1. Wash onions and peel them.
2. Chop or slice the onions. Alternatively, the onions can be diced.
3. Place the onions in the fermenting vessel.
4. Fill the vessel with brine. Leave room for the weight. Get rid of any air bubbles that form in the container.

5. Add the starter culture now, if you're going to add it.
6. Place the weight into the vessel and press it down. The weight should be below the surface of the brine. Add more brine, if necessary. Leave 1" of headspace.
7. Place the lid on the container and seal it.
8. Let the container ferment in an area with an ambient temperature as close to 72° F as you can get. Burp the container once a day.

Fermenting time:

Onions should be allowed to ferment for 7 to 10 days. Start checking them after 7 days and move the container to cold storage once the onions have fermented to your preference.

Parsnips

Parsnips are a root vegetable that look similar to a carrot, except they're cream-colored. They're used in a manner similar to carrots, but they have a sweeter flavor. They contain a balanced profile of vitamins and minerals and are a good source of fiber. They're a good candidate for fermenting, as it balances out their sweetness and gives them a sweet and sour flavor that pairs nicely with soups and salads.

Selection:

Small to medium parsnips are best for fermenting because they aren't as fibrous as larger parsnips. Choose firm parsnips with smooth, taut skin.

Ingredients:

4 to 6 parsnips.

2 tablespoons sea salt.

Filtered water.

Starter Culture:

Starter culture is optional in this recipe. You can use ¼ cup of whey, a packet of vegetable starter culture or a few tablespoons of liquid from a previous ferment.

Instructions:

1. Wash and peel the parsnips.
2. Shred them into thin slices.
3. Place the parsnips into the fermenting vessel.

4. Fill the vessel with brine. Leave room for the weight. Get rid of any air bubbles that form in the container.
5. Add the starter culture now, if you're going to add it.
6. Place the weight into the vessel and press it down. The weight should be below the surface of the brine. Add more brine, if necessary. Leave 1" of headspace.
7. Place the lid on the container and seal it.
8. Let the container ferment in an area with an ambient temperature as close to 72° F as you can get. Burp the container once a day.

Fermenting time:

Ferment parsnips for 4 to 7 days. Start checking them after the 4th day and move them to cold storage once they've fermented to your liking.

Cultured Pesto

This pesto isn't quite as thick as regular pesto because of the amount of brine used to ferment it, but it still makes a great addition to soups, pasta dishes and salads. Make sure you add it to your dishes after cooking them because the heat generated during cooking will kill the beneficial bacteria in the pasta.

Selection:

Use fresh basil that is undamaged and hasn't started to wilt.

Ingredients:

4 cups basil leaves.

4 garlic cloves.

¼ cup pine nuts.

2 tablespoons lime juice.

3 tablespoons sea salt.

Filtered water.

Starter Culture:

Starter culture isn't necessary for this recipe.

Instructions:

1. Wash the basil.
2. If the basil has thick stems, remove the stems. Thin stems can be left alone and processed.
3. Peel the garlic cloves.
4. Add the basil leaves, garlic cloves, pine nuts, lime juice and 1 tablespoon of sea salt to a

blender or food processor and process until the pesto is the consistency you desire.

5. Place the pesto into the fermenting vessel.
6. Create brine by mixing the remaining 2 tablespoons of sea salt with 4 cups of water. Pour the brine over the pesto and let it seep down into the pesto. The brine should fill any air pockets in the pesto. Cover the pesto with at least an inch of brine. Leave 1" to 2" of headspace in the container.
7. Place the lid on the container and seal it.
8. Let the container ferment in an area with an ambient temperature as close to 72° F as you can get.

Fermenting time:

Let the pesto ferment for 3 to 5 days before moving it to cold storage.

Cultured Pickles

You'd be hard-pressed to find pickles at your local supermarket that contain active bacterial cultures. Most pickles are pickled in vinegar and have been pasteurized to kill off all bacteria, both good and bad. These pickles taste similar to the ones you get in the store, but have a bit more tang to them. The upside is they're full of probiotic bacteria.

Selection:

Select medium cucumbers that are green and crisp.

Ingredients:

3 to 4 medium cucumbers.

3 tablespoons fresh dill leaves.

1 tablespoon dill seeds.

2 cloves garlic.

5 peppercorns.

2 tablespoons sea salt.

4 cups filtered water.

Starter Culture:

Starter culture can be used, but it isn't necessary. Use a couple tablespoons of liquid from a previous ferment or a packet of starter culture for best results.

Instructions:

1. Wash the cucumbers. Cut them into slices that are a couple inches shorter than the jar they'll be fermented in.
2. Quarter the cucumbers by cutting them in half lengthwise and then cutting the pieces in half again.
3. Cut away the seeds.
4. Peel the garlic cloves. Cut them into pieces and mash them up.
5. Place the cucumber slices into the fermenting vessel(s).
6. Place the garlic in the container(s). If more than one container is used, divide the garlic between the containers.
7. Combine the sea salt and water to create brine.
8. Pour the brine over the top of the cucumbers. Make sure the cucumbers are completely submerged. Leave room for the weight. Remove any visible air bubbles.
9. Add the starter culture to each jar, if you're going to going to use it.
10. Divide the dill leaves, dill seeds and peppercorns amongst the containers.
11. Place a weight in the container. Add more brine, if necessary to submerge the weight. Leave an inch or two of headspace.
12. Seal each container following the manufacturer's instructions.
13. Leave the container(s) to ferment at room temperature.

Fermenting time:

It can take up to a week for cucumbers to ferment. Taste them after three days and continue tasting them daily until they've fermented to your liking.

Probiotic Salad

There no doubt that eating salad is good for you, as long as you don't drench it with salad dressing. Probiotic salad is even better for you than regular salad—and you don't need to add any salad dressing to it. It's good on its own. Feel free to add and remove vegetables from this salad to suit your tastes.

Selection:

Choose vegetables that are undamaged and prime for eating.

Ingredients:

1 head of cabbage.

1 red bell pepper.

1 green bell pepper.

1 carrot.

1 medium onion.

1 teaspoon ginger.

2 tablespoons sea salt.

Filtered water.

Starter Culture:

Starter culture can be added, but it isn't mandatory. ¼ cup of whey will get this recipe off to a good start.

Instructions:

1. Wash the vegetables.
2. Core the cabbage and chop it into thin slices.

3. Place the cabbage in a large bowl and add the sea salt to it. Mash the cabbage with a kraut hammer.
4. Cut the bell peppers in half and remove the seeds and cores. Slice the bell peppers into thin slices.
5. Peel the carrot and slice it into thin slices.
6. Peel the onion and slice it.
7. Add bell peppers, onion and the carrot slices to the bowl and stir them in.
8. Cover the bowl and let the bowl sit in the fridge overnight. The vegetables should release enough juice to create brine that can be used to pack the fermented vegetables in.
9. Place the vegetables in the fermenting vessel, along with the brine. There should be enough brine to cover the vegetables. If not, more brine can be made by adding a tablespoon of sea salt to 2 cups of water. Add brine until the vegetables are completely covered.
10. If you're using starter culture, add it to the vessel now.
11. Get rid of any air bubbles that form. Add more brine if necessary.
12. Place a weight in the container and press it down so the vegetables are submersed below the surface of the brine. Leave a 1" to 2" headspace at the top of the container.
13. Seal the container. The method used to seal the container varies from container to container, so check the directions that came with your container.

14. Place the container in a dark area of your house with an ambient temperature of around 72° F. Let the vegetables ferment until they've fermented to your liking.

Fermenting time:

Probiotic salad should be fermented for 3 to 5 days and then moved to cold storage.

Cultured Salsa

Cultured salsa can be used the same way you would normally use regular salsa, plus it has an extended shelf life. Store this salsa in the fridge and it'll last months, as opposed to regular salsa, which goes bad in a couple days. You probably won't have to worry about shelf life though, as this salsa will disappear from the fridge shortly after it's made.

The only applications not recommended for this salsa are recipes where the salsa is heated or cooked. Cooking this salsa will kill off the probiotic bacteria. It's fine to eat it cooked, but cooking it sort of defeats the purpose.

Selection:

Choose ripe peppers that are firm to the touch. Do not use peppers with visible damage or soft spots.

Ingredients:

12 serrano peppers.

2 jalapeno peppers.

4 cherry peppers.

OPTIONAL: 1 habanero pepper.

5 medium carrots.

1 red bell pepper.

1 onion.

5 garlic cloves.

2 tablespoons fresh shredded ginger.

3 tablespoons sea salt.

Filtered water.

Starter Culture:

Yes. Use ¼ cup of whey.

Instructions:

1. Wash the peppers and remove the stems.
2. Chop the peppers into coarse chunks.
3. Place the peppers in a bowl and stir the sea salt into them.
4. Wash and peel the carrots. Shred the carrots.
5. Wash the bell pepper. Cut it in half and remove the core and the seeds. Chop it into coarse chunks.
6. Peel the onion and dice it.
7. Peel and mince the garlic cloves.
8. Add all of the vegetables to the bowl. Mix them together.
9. Place the vegetables and any liquid in the bowl into the fermenting vessel.
10. Fill the jar to within 2" of the top with filtered water.
11. Add ¼ cup of whey to the vessel.
12. Place the lid on the container and seal it.
13. Let the container ferment in an area with an ambient temperature as close to 72° F as you can get.

Fermenting time:

Cultured salsa should be allowed to ferment for 3 to 5 days before it's moved into cold storage.

Sauerkraut

This is the recipe most people start off when they embark on their fermenting journey. Sauerkraut is one of the easier recipes to ferment because all you need is salt and cabbage. You can use starter culture if you'd like, but cabbage contains all the cultures you need to get started.

Sauerkraut is typically used as a condiment for other foods. It's mainly used on meat dishes and is a popular topping for hot dogs.

Selection:

Use freshly harvested heads of cabbage. Do not use cabbage that has started to wilt or has browning leaf ends. Various types of cabbage can be used. For an interesting visual effect, combine different colors of cabbage.

Ingredients:

4 heads of cabbage.

3 tablespoons of sea salt.

Starter Culture:

Starter culture can be used, but isn't absolutely necessary because cabbage has a high level of beneficial bacteria.

Instructions:

1. Wash the heads of cabbage.
2. Chop the heads of cabbage up into tiny pieces. A blender or food processor can be used for this step.
3. Place the cabbage in a bowl and bruise it with a kraut hammer. This is a blunt object used to

bruise cabbage to help it release moisture. If you don't have a kraut hammer, any blunt object will do.

4. As you chop each head of cabbage and bruise it, add sea salt to the cabbage.

5. Cover the bowl and let it sit in the fridge overnight.

6. In the morning, you should find the cabbage has released a lot of moisture. If fresh cabbage was used, you will usually have enough natural brine to pack the cabbage in without having to add more brine. If brine does need to be added, you can make brine by combining a level tablespoon of salt with a quart of water.

7. Place the salted cabbage in the fermenting vessel. Pack it in tightly. Leave room at the top of the container for the weight and a couple inches of headspace. Remove any air bubbles in the cabbage.

8. Place the weight in the vessel and press it down. The weight should be below the surface of the brine. If there isn't enough brine, make some and add it to the container.

9. Place the lid on the container and let it sit at room temperature for 12 hours. Remove the lid and press the weight down into the sauerkraut again.

10. Place the lid back on the container and seal it so it's airtight. The method of doing this is dependent on the type of container being used.

P a g e |**111**

Consult the manufacturer's instructions that came with the fermenting vessel.

11. Let the container ferment in an area with an ambient temperature as close to 72° F as you can get. Let the sauerkraut ferment until it has fermented to your liking. Don't forget to burp airtight containers every couple of days.

Fermenting Time:

How long you let sauerkraut ferment is a matter of personal taste. Some people like their kraut fermented for only a few days, while others advocate letting it ferment for a month or longer. What I suggest is letting it ferment for a few days the first time and then taste-testing it. Continue tasting it every couple days until it has fermented to your preference.

Spicy Red Sauerkraut

This sauerkraut is red because red cabbage is used in the recipe. It can just as easily be made with any other color of cabbage or a blend of different colors of cabbage. The jalapenos give it a spicy kick. They can be eliminated or replaced with more carrots if you don't like spicy foods.

Selection:

Use freshly harvested heads of cabbage. Do not use cabbage that has started to wilt or has browning leaf ends. Select carrots that are straight and firm to the touch and jalapenos that are also firm.

Ingredients:

2 heads of red cabbage.

2 to 3 tablespoons sea salt.

3 medium jalapenos.

2 medium carrots.

Starter Culture:

Starter culture can be used, but isn't necessary.

Instructions:

1. Wash the cabbage.
2. Chop the heads of cabbage up into tiny pieces. A blender or food processor can be used for this step.
3. Place the cabbage into a bowl and press it with a kraut hammer. If you don't have a kraut hammer, any blunt object will do.

4. As you chop each head of cabbage and bruise it, add sea salt to the cabbage.

5. Cover the bowl and let it sit in the fridge overnight.

6. In the morning, you should find the cabbage has released a lot of moisture. If fresh cabbage was used, you will usually have enough natural brine to pack the cabbage in without having to add more brine.

7. Wash the jalapenos and carrots.

8. Cut the jalapenos in half and remove the seeds. Dice the jalapenos and add them to the bowl with the cabbage.

9. Peel the carrots and shred them.

10. Mix the carrots and jalapenos into the shredded cabbage.

11. Place the salted cabbage, jalapenos and the shredded carrots into the fermenting vessel(s). Pack them in tightly. Leave room at the top of the container for the weight and a couple inches of headspace. Remove any air bubbles that form.

12. Place the weight in the vessel and press it down. The weight should be below the surface of the brine. If there isn't enough brine, make some and add it to the container. If brine does need to be added, you can make brine by combining a level tablespoon or two of sea salt with a quart of water.

13. Place the lid on the container and let it sit at room temperature for 12 hours. Remove the lid

and press the weight down into the sauerkraut again.

14. Place the lid back on the container and seal it so it's airtight. The method of doing this is dependent on the type of container being used. Consult the manufacturer's instructions that came with the fermenting vessel.

15. Let the container ferment in an area with an ambient temperature as close to 72° F as you can get. Let the sauerkraut ferment until it has fermented to your liking. Don't forget to burp airtight containers every couple of days.

Fermenting time:

This sauerkraut really starts to come into its own after a week or two of fermenting time. Taste it after a week and then again every few days after that until it has fermented to your liking.

Caraway Apple Kraut

I was really hesitant to try this recipe when it was given to me by a friend. Apple and sauerkraut were two items I'd never considered mixing and I wasn't sure how the flavors would blend. I have to admit I was pleasantly surprised. The caraway adds another level of flavor that takes this sauerkraut over the top.

Selection:

Use freshly harvested heads of cabbage. Do not use cabbage that has started to wilt or has browning leaf ends. Choose green apples that have just started to ripen and are firm to the touch.

Ingredients:

4 heads of cabbage.

1 carrot.

2 green apples.

3 tablespoons sea salt.

Starter Culture:

Starter culture isn't necessary because of the cabbage, but you can use it if you'd like.

Instructions:

1. Wash the heads of cabbage.
2. Chop the heads of cabbage up into tiny pieces. A blender or food processor can be used for this step.

3. Place the cabbage in a bowl and press it with a kraut hammer. If you don't have a kraut hammer, any blunt object will do.
4. As you chop each head of cabbage up and bruise it, add sea salt to the cabbage.
5. Cover the bowl and let it sit in the fridge overnight.
6. In the morning, you should find the cabbage has released a lot of moisture. If fresh cabbage was used, you will usually have enough natural brine to pack the cabbage without having to add more brine. If brine does need to be added, you can make brine by combining a level tablespoon or two of salt with a quart of water.
7. Wash the apples and the carrot and peel them. Core the apples and chop them into small pieces. Shred the carrot.
8. Place the shredded carrot and chopped apple pieces in the bowl with the cabbage and mix them in thoroughly.
9. Place the sauerkraut in the fermenting vessel. Pack it in tightly. Leave room at the top of the container for the weight. Remove any air bubbles in the cabbage.
10. Place the weight in the vessel and press it down. The weight should be below the surface of the brine. If there isn't enough brine, make some and add it to the container. Leave a couple inches of headspace in the container.
11. Place the lid on the container and let it sit at room temperature for 12 hours. Remove the lid

and press the weight down into the sauerkraut again.

12. Place the lid back on the container and seal it so it's airtight. The method of doing this is dependent on the type of container being used. Consult the manufacturer's instructions that came with the fermenting vessel.

13. Let the container ferment in an area with an ambient temperature as close to 72° F as you can get. Let the sauerkraut ferment until it has fermented to your liking. Don't forget to burp airtight containers every couple of days.

Fermenting time:

This sauerkraut is usually at its best after a 4 to 6 week fermenting period.

Ginger Carrot Kraut

Here's another tasty sauerkraut variation. Ginger adds an interesting flair to this otherwise ordinary sauerkraut. I use a combination of red and green cabbage for this recipe to give it an interesting touch of color. The addition of the carrots adds a bit of sweetness and even more color.

Selection:

Use freshly harvested heads of cabbage. Do not use cabbage that has started to wilt or has browning leaf ends. Select mature carrots that are firm to the touch.

Ingredients:

2 heads of green cabbage.

2 heads of red cabbage.

5 medium carrots.

3 tablespoons grated ginger.

3 tablespoons sea salt.

2 tablespoons caraway seeds.

Starter Culture:

Starter culture can be added to this recipe if you'd like, but it isn't a necessity. The cabbage has plenty of bacterial cultures to get fermentation started. If you do add starter culture, a culture packet or a couple tablespoons of liquid from a previous ferment are both good choices.

Instructions:

1. Wash the cabbage and shred it. Place the shredded cabbage in a bowl. As you finish each

head of cabbage, sprinkle sea salt on top and pound it with a kraut hammer.

2. Wash the carrots and shred them. Add the carrots to the bowl.
3. Stir in the ginger and the caraway seeds.
4. Cover the bowl and let it sit overnight. In the morning, the cabbage should have released enough moisture to create enough brine to cover the sauerkraut. If not, you can make brine by adding 2 tablespoons of sea salt to a quart of water.
5. Place the sauerkraut into the fermenting vessel. Pack it in as tightly as you can get it. Remove any visible air bubbles.
6. Press the weight down into the vessel. The brine should be over the top of the weight and the sauerkraut should be held beneath the surface of the brine by the weight. Add more brine if necessary. Leave a 1" to 2" headspace at the top of the container.
7. Seal the container. The method used to seal the container varies from container to container, so check the directions that came with your container.
8. Place the sauerkraut in a dark area of your house with an ambient temperature of around 72° F. Let the sauerkraut ferment until it has fermented to your liking. Don't forget to burp airtight containers every couple of days.

Fermenting time:

This sauerkraut should be ready within 2 to 3 weeks. Check it after 2 weeks and then every couple of days until it has fermented to your liking.

Cultured Sauerkraut Coleslaw

This isn't a fermenting recipe. It's a recipe you can make from sauerkraut to create tasty fermented coleslaw. If you like coleslaw, you'll probably love this cultured version of it.

Selection:

Use regular sauerkraut that has shredded carrots in it for this recipe.

Ingredients:

3 cups sauerkraut.

¼ cup mayonnaise.

1 tablespoon maple syrup.

¼ teaspoon black pepper.

Instructions:

1. Combine all of the ingredients in a bowl and stir them together.
2. Serve right away.

Cherry Tomatoes

This recipe is a great way to preserve an abundant cherry tomato harvest while adding probiotic bacteria to them. These tomatoes can be used the same way you'd use regular cherry tomatoes, but keep in mind cooking them will kill the beneficial bacteria.

Selection:

Choose cherry tomatoes that have been freshly harvested. They should be red and ripe and the skins should be taut.

Ingredients:

2 to 3 pounds of cherry tomatoes.

2 cloves garlic.

¼ cup green onions, diced.

1 tablespoon sea salt.

Filtered water.

Starter Culture:

Yes. A packet of vegetable starter culture or liquid from a previous ferment can be used as starter culture for this recipe.

Instructions:

1. Wash the tomatoes and remove the stems.
2. Peel the garlic cloves.
3. Fill the fermenting vessel with tomatoes.
4. Add the garlic cloves, onions and sea salt to the container.

5. Add the starter culture to the vessel.
6. Fill the vessel with water. Leave room for the weight. Get rid of any air bubbles that form in the container.
7. Place the weight into the vessel and press it down. The weight should be below the surface of the brine. Add more water, if necessary. Leave 1" of headspace.
8. Place the lid on the container and seal it.
9. Let the container ferment in an area with an ambient temperature as close to 72° F as you can get. Burp airtight containers once a day.

Fermenting time:

Cherry tomatoes should be left to ferment for 4 to 7 days. Check them once a day after the 4th day and move them to the fridge once they've fermented to your liking.

Green Tomatoes

For the sake of clarity, the green tomatoes used in this recipe are unripe tomatoes that are harvested before the tomatoes ripen on the vine. For many, green tomatoes are a source of frustration, because there always seems to be at least some tomatoes that are particularly stubborn when it comes to ripening. I used to dread green tomatoes, because one can only handle so many fried green tomatoes. Now, I look forward to green tomatoes because these fermented tomatoes are a delicious treat.

Selection:

Choose green tomatoes that haven't yet started to ripen. The tomatoes should be completely green for this recipe.

Ingredients:

15 to 20 cherry tomatoes.

2 garlic cloves.

2 tablespoons dill seeds.

2 tablespoons sea salt.

Starter Culture:

Yes. Use ¼ cup of whey or a packet of vegetable starter culture.

Instructions:

1. Wash the tomatoes and remove the stems.
2. Fill the fermenting vessel with tomatoes.
3. Add the garlic, dill seeds and salt to the container.

4. Add ¼ cup of whey or a packet of vegetable starter culture to the vessel.
5. Fill the vessel with water. Leave room for the weight. Get rid of any air bubbles that form in the container.
6. Place the weight into the vessel and press it down. The weight should be below the surface of the brine. Add more water, if necessary. Leave 1" of headspace.
7. Place the lid on the container and seal it.
8. Let the container ferment in an area with an ambient temperature as close to 72° F as you can get.

Fermenting time:

Green tomatoes should be left to ferment for 2 to 4 days before being moved to the fridge.

Green Tomato Salsa

Here's another use for green tomatoes. You can use them to make a tasty salsa. I would classify this salsa as medium heat. It has a bit of kick to it, but isn't too bad. It gets milder if you let it sit in the fridge for a week or two after the fermentation period. If you want milder salsa, eliminate some of the peppers. Those looking for more kick can add a habanero pepper or two.

Selection:

Choose green tomatoes that haven't yet started to ripen. You want tomatoes that are completely green for this recipe.

Ingredients:

8 to 10 green tomatoes.

1 ripe tomato.

1 medium onion.

4 jalapeno peppers.

3 banana peppers.

3 cloves garlic.

¾ cup cilantro, chopped.

4 tablespoons lemon juice.

2 tablespoons salt.

2 tablespoons apple cider vinegar.

Starter Culture:

Yes. Use ¼ cup of whey, starter culture from a previous ferment or a packet of vegetable starter culture.

Instructions:

1. Wash the tomatoes and peppers and remove the stems.
2. Peel the onions and garlic.
3. Add all of the ingredients to a blender or food processor and blend it until it reaches the desired consistency.
4. Transfer the salsa to the fermenting vessel. Get rid of any air bubbles that form. Leave 1" to 2" of headspace in the container.
5. Place the lid on the container and seal it.
6. Let the container ferment in an area with an ambient temperature as close to 72° F as you can get. Burp the container at least once a day.

Fermenting time:

Green tomato salsa should be left to ferment for up to a week before being moved to the fridge.

Lacto-Turnips

Turnips are a member of the radish family. Like other members of this family, turnips contain bitter compounds that give them a bit of kick when they're bitten into. Fermenting turnips helps eliminate some of this kick and it evens out the flavor a bit.

Selection:

Select turnips that are on the small side. Smaller turnips aren't as "hot" as larger turnips.

Ingredients:

10 to 15 turnips.

2 tablespoons sea salt.

Filtered water.

Starter Culture:

This simple recipe only requires turnips and brine. Starter culture can be added, but isn't necessary.

Instructions:

1. Wash the turnips and remove the stems.
2. Slice the turnips into thin slices.
3. Fill the fermenting vessel with turnip slices.
4. Create brine by combining 4 cups of filtered water with 2 tablespoons of sea salt.
5. Add the starter culture now, if you're going to add it.
6. Fill the vessel with brine. Leave room for the weight. Get rid of any air bubbles that form in the container.

7. Place the weight into the vessel and press it down. The weight should be below the surface of the brine. Add more brine, if necessary. Leave 1" of headspace.
8. Place the lid on the container and seal it.
9. Let the container ferment in an area with an ambient temperature as close to 72° F as you can get. Burp the container once a day.

Fermenting time:

Turnips should be allowed to ferment for up to a week. Move them to cold storage once they've fermented to your liking.

Cultured Vegetable Mix

Here's a tasty mix of cultured vegetables that features cauliflower, carrots and kale. The salt, onions, garlic and the spice blend all combine to create a flavor that's tough to beat. Feel free to add or remove vegetables from this mixture to suit your tastes. You can also adjust the spices to your liking.

Selection:

Use undamaged cauliflower florets with tightly packed heads. The carrots should be undamaged medium-sized carrots that are prime for eating. Avoid older carrots that have gotten too fibrous. The kale leaves should be fresh and unwilted.

Ingredients:

4 cups cauliflower florets.

3 medium carrots.

1 onion.

½ cup kale leaves.

2 cloves garlic.

10 peppercorns.

½ teaspoon curry powder.

2 tablespoons sea salt.

Filtered water.

Starter Culture:

Starter culture can be used with this recipe to get it off to a good start. A starter culture packet, a few tablespoons of juice from a previous ferment or ¼ cup of whey are all good choices.

Instructions:

1. Wash the vegetables.
2. Break the cauliflower florets up into small 1" to 2" pieces.
3. Peel the carrots and slice them into coins.
4. Peel the onion and dice it.
5. Wash the kale and chop it into 2" to 3" pieces. Remove any large stems.
6. Peel the garlic and chop it into small pieces.
7. Place the vegetables into the fermenting vessel(s) in layers.
8. Create brine by mixing 2 tablespoons of sea salt with 4 cups of filtered water.
9. Add the peppercorns and curry powder to the brine and stir them in.
10. Cover the vegetables with the brine. Remove any air bubbles that form.
11. Add the starter culture to the fermenting vessel(s).
12. Press the weight down into the vessel(s). The weight should be submerged beneath the surface of the brine.
13. Add more brine if necessary. Leave 1" to 2" of headspace at the top of the container.
14. Seal the container. The method used to seal the container varies from container to container, so

check the directions that came with your
container.

15. Place the container in a dark area of your house
with an ambient temperature of around 72° F.
Let the vegetables ferment until they have
fermented to your liking. Don't forget to burp
airtight containers every couple of days.

Fermenting time:

This recipe takes 4 to 7 days to ferment. Begin tasting
the vegetables after the 4th day.

Curried Zucchini

This recipe calls for curry powder. If you don't care for the curry powder, you can eliminate the curry and simply ferment the zucchini and sea salt. If you want to switch things up a bit, this recipe will work with other thin-skinned squash, too. Try combining different squash types for an interesting look and flavor blend.

Selection:

Select 6" to 8" zucchini that are firm to the touch and free of damage.

Ingredients:

4 to 6 zucchini.

4 cloves organic garlic.

3 to 4 tablespoons curry powder.

2 tablespoons sea salt.

Filtered water.

Starter Culture:

Starter culture is optional with this recipe. If you want to add it, use ¼ cup of whey, 3 tablespoons of liquid from a previous ferment or a packet of vegetable starter culture.

Instructions:

1. Wash the zucchini and slice the zucchini into coins.
2. Peel and mince the garlic cloves.
3. Add the zucchini and garlic cloves to the fermenting vessel.

4. Create brine by combining 4 cups of filtered water with 2 tablespoons of sea salt.
5. Add the curry powder and stir it in.
6. Add the starter culture now, if you're going to add it.
7. Fill the vessel with brine. Leave room for the weight. Get rid of any air bubbles that form in the container.
8. Place the weight into the vessel and press it down. The weight should be below the surface of the brine. Add more brine, if necessary. Leave 1" of headspace.
9. Place the lid on the container and seal it.
10. Let the container ferment in an area with an ambient temperature as close to 72° F as you can get. Burp the container once a day.

Fermenting time:

Let zucchini ferment for 2 to 3 days. Watch it closely because it will go soft quickly.

Common Problems Encountered During Fermenting

There are a number of common problems you may encounter when fermenting vegetables. Let's take a quick look at some of the more common problems encountered during fermentation and what can be done to avoid and/or solve each problem.

Mold

Mold is a fairly common occurrence in fermented foods. There are a wide variety of molds that can grow on foods, most of which are completely harmless. The problem with mold is there are a handful of molds that are toxic to humans and it's almost impossible to tell the different types of mold apart unless you're a scientist examining them under a microscope.

Some fermentation experts recommend removing the food on top that has mold growing on it and keeping the food below that still looks fine. The problem with this line of thinking is mold sends out invisible tendrils as it grows, so the food below the obviously moldy food may be infected with mold and hasn't yet started to show visible signs.

I know this goes against conventional thinking, but I usually throw out moldy batches of fermented foods. I'd rather be safe than sorry. To prevent mold from forming in the first place, keep vegetables submerged completely beneath the surface of the brine and use containers that don't allow air inside.

Vegetables that Don't Ferment

Sometimes you'll get a batch of vegetables that just won't ferment. This is more common with wild fermentation than it is when starter cultures are added because the natural bacteria on vegetables are more susceptible to environmental variables. Adding starter culture ensures there are ample amounts of good bacteria in the fermenting vessel, which is usually enough to get the vegetables headed in the right direction.

Some batches take a longer time to ferment than others, so don't give up too early. If it's cooler than the recommended fermenting temperature or starter cultures weren't used, the fermentation process can take a few days to pick up steam.

Too much salt can also hinder fermentation. 2 to 3 tablespoons of salt per quart of water is all you need to create good brine for fermenting vegetables in. Any more than that and you run the risk of stopping the fermentation process or slowing it down to the point that it feels like it's stopped. If you think you may have added too much salt, dilute the brine by pouring some of the brine out and adding water. Starter culture can be added when you dilute the brine to try and get things headed in the right direction.

Slime

Slimy brine or a slimy coating on the vegetables is an indicator something is very wrong. The slime is a byproduct that comes from microorganisms that produce slime. This means the wrong types of microorganisms are growing in your vegetables and it's time to throw out the batch and start over.

Slime-producing microorganisms can take control for a number of reasons. Not using enough salt in the brine and leaving air bubbles in the container when you add the brine are two of the more common reasons.

Cloudy Substance at Top of Brine

At times, a milky white substance may start to form at the top of the brine. This substance is usually harmless yeast that can be skimmed off and thrown out. Remove as much of the yeast as you can and replace any lost brine and the fermented vegetables should be good to go.

Vegetables Smell Rotten

If you open the fermenting vessel and are hit with a rotting stench instead of a sour smell, do not eat the vegetables inside the container. Food that smells rotten has gone bad and you can get very ill from eating this food.

There's an unmistakable difference between food that smells sour and food that smells rotten, but the difference may not be clear when you first start fermenting food. If there's ever any doubt as to whether fermented vegetables have gone bad, it's best to err on the side of caution. Throw them out and make a new batch.

Strange Tastes

Fermenting is a symbiotic process that involves a lot of variables. No two ferments will taste exactly the same because the bacterial cultures act differently in every ferment. You can ferment three batches of vegetables in a row and do everything exactly the same and all three will likely have subtle differences in taste and texture. That's just the nature of the beast when it comes to fermented food.

If you have a batch that isn't appealing to you for one reason or another, throw it out and try again. If you didn't use starter culture, try using starter culture. If you did use starter culture, try a different kind of starter culture. You can also try more or less salt and you can add and remove spices to switch up the flavor.

If a batch tastes like it's gone bad, throw it out. Taste is your last line of defense against spoiled food. Never eat anything that doesn't taste right to you.

Soft Vegetables

All vegetables will eventually go soft if left to ferment for a lengthy period of time. Different vegetables go soft at different rates of speed. Some will start to go soft after a day or two of fermenting, while others will take weeks or even months. Vegetables left to ferment for too long will eventually turn to mush. This is part of the natural fermentation process.

To slow down softening and keep vegetables crisp for a longer period of time, add a grape leaf or two to the container before you set it out to ferment. The tannin in the grape leaf will help keep the vegetables crisp. Adding salt to the brine also helps keep vegetables crisp, but be careful not to add too much.

Monitor your vegetables closely while they're fermenting and move them to cold storage before they go soft. Once they've gone soft, there's nothing you can do to bring them back.

Foam in Brine

The carbon dioxide created during fermentation will often create foam at the top of the brine as it bubbles to the surface. Sweeter vegetables usually foam up more than vegetables with low sugar content. This foam is a natural part of the fermenting process and should go away within a couple days.

Other Books You May Be Interested In

Volume 1 of the Recipes in a Jar series covers canning fruit:

http://www.amazon.com/Recipes-Jar-How-Fruit-ebook/dp/B00GCA7OUG/

Vol. 2 of the Recipes in a Jar series covers canning vegetables:

http://www.amazon.com/Recipes-Jar-vol-How-Vegetables-ebook/dp/B00GGMDP94/

Learn how to dry fruit with part one in this series:

http://www.amazon.com/Food-Drying-vol-Fruit-
ebook/dp/B00FN6JFRU/

COMPREHENSIVE CHI-GONG MANUAL

Easily Relatable, Accessible & Digestible Chi-Gong Education.

Authored by:
REES DUNN

Digitally Designed by:
REES DUNN

CONTENTS:

OUR MISSION:

MAKING CHI-GONG
RELATABLE, ACCESSIBLE & DIGESTABLE

BETTER CHI-GONG EDUCATION

21ST CENTURY PEOPLE MAKING ANCIENT GEMS USEFUL FOR 21ST CENTURY PEOPLE

JOIN THE BETTER CHI-GONG EDUCATION CENTER & BECOME THE FULLY EMBODIED PRACTITIONER YOU'VE ALWAYS DREAMED

IF YOU'VE ALWAYS DREAMED OF HAVING RAZOR SHARP FOCUS, LONG ATTENTION SPAN OR BEING SUPREMELY AND DIVINELY CONNECTED TO NATURE THEN YOU HAVE COME TO THE RIGHT PLACE.

THOUSANDS OF PEOPLE HAVE RELIED ON REES' COACHING FOR THE GUIDANCE, TOOLS AND RESOURCES NEEDED TO TAKE THEIR HEALTH, THEIR MENTAL, EMOTIONAL AND SPIRITUAL PRACTICE TO A HIGHER PLACE FASTER THAN EVER IMAGINED.

FROM IMPROVED HAPPINESS TO DEEPER BREATHS OR EVEN SENSING SHARPER WITH PINPOINT ACCURACY TO THE SKILLS TO TRANSMUTE NEGATIVITY INTO POSITIVITY. WHATEVER YOUR INTENTION, OUR COURSES AND COACHING SERVICES CAN HELP YOU.

WWW.BETTERCHIGONG.EDUCATION.COM

 REES.THE.FLAME@GMAIL.COM

 @REES.THE.FLAME

BETTER CHI-GONG EDUCATION
21ST CENTURY PEOPLE MAKING ANCIENT GEMS USEFUL FOR 21ST CENTURY PEOPLE

Authors Note:

When I began writing this book. I knew already, I am not the only one to make a book about chi-gong. Without a doubt I knew what I was about to write was, is and will always be necessary for chi-gong to remain a loved practice.

The reason I wrote this book is not to prove anything. Not to prove Chi-gong is superior than yoga. Not to prove Chi-gong is great for the elderly & even not to prove how powerful Chigong is for workplace stress management. I wrote this book to bring clarity to the common western misunderstanding, of this TCM (Traditional Chinese Medicine) practice. You see, I noticed Chi-gong being taught in a way that is secretive to the beginner. In a way that the beginner has to prove themselves to receive the treasures of the practice. Which can take years upon years. I Believe this dated mindset is regressive for these times. I take responsibility to pioneer a new digestible way to transfer the knowledgeable, wisdom and inner/over standing of Chi-gong Practice.

Truly, Chi/Qi or Universal energy is a gift for all of us that can be shared to help heal others. Neither money nor material goods are needed; only willing hands, a willing mind, and the knowledge of the natural healing power of Nature.

Acknowledgements:

No journey can take place except in the presence of the supreme God. What is God to me? God is love, unendingly. God is an undeniable force! Any of the names of the supreme are respected by me. Allah, Jah, Gye Nyame, the universe and all the names of God that fit right for people of the earth from different walks of life.

God gifts us on the journey with people and things. Even gifts us mess and messengers.

Let's begin,

Extending My Great Fortune to have supportive parents around the unconventional life I have and am still grateful to be living.

Extending My Gratitude to the Chi-gong, Martial arts and Combat Mentors that have blessed me thus far:

Ali Al Sarraf
Neville Obodai Tetteh
Benjamin Cullen
Kenneth Jarvis
Ben and Craig Houstan
Bader Alotaibi
Mark Wynter

Extending my Grace to those who granted me opportunity to share my gifts:
Aj Haast
Rachel Cox
Lisa Cuerdan
Tracy Morgan
Majesty Rain
Ben & Craig Houston

Extending my gratitude to YOU, the reader, who invested in this book. Thankyou for your authentic interest and supporting the journey.

CHAPTER 1:

CHI-GONG
ENCAPSULATED

WHAT DOES CHI-GONG MEAN?

CHI-GONG

(PRONOUNCED CHEE-GUNG)

CHI means vital energy, breath or spirit.

GONG means "the voyage to mastery", "the endless pursuit of better" or simply "to build".

MASTERY OF YOUR ENERGY

or in other words...

BUILD YOUR ENERGY

WHAT IS CHI-GONG?

Chi-Gong is a health exercise for maintaining and improving health.

This method can be recognised for healing more than 4,000 years ago & is a branch of Traditional Chinese Medicine. One of the world's oldest and most effective healing systems, Chinese medicine is responsible for the discovery of such successfully proven therapies as acupuncture and acupressure.

According to Chinese medicine, in addition to the physical structures of your body, you also have physical energy that is constantly circulating through every cell of your body. Over the millennia and now, thousands of people have practiced and continue to improve health using this natural method that does not require any material objects to effect a profound improvement in health.

The 2 components of Chi-Gong are:

Chi Exercise

Chi Meditation

WHAT IS CHI EXERCISE?

Chi-gong Exercise is fundamentally an open eyed movement meditation experience. Generally done standing, suitable to do without any equipment and can be done anywhere. An inner experience of appreciating the outer world which can have infinite layers of bliss to explore. Chi exercise is especially enhanced when practiced; Outside; in the sun; under the moon and stars; by fire; by flowing water; with trees; stood on tree stumps, and more. As you build your foundation in Chi Exercise, consciously, you'll begin to pulse Chi energy outwards into your environment or bring it inwards from your environment to store the energy. This Vital energy is moved through a profound slow breathing and movement technique coupled together with neuro-acoustics; tapping; meridian acupressure.

WHAT IS CHI MEDITATION?

Chi-Gong Meditation is a stillness practice which focuses on Dan-Tien Breathing. Can be done in standing postures, on a chair seated or on the floor seated. The focus is to bring your attentive awareness deeper & deeper into the core of your essence. Also, to release your body of all it's holdings and let the natural gravitational drop happen through you. Chi Meditation is a health exercise for maintain and improving health.

WHAT IS YIN AND YANG?

In Ancient Chinese philosophy, yin and yang is a concept of dualism, describing how obviously opposite or contrary forces may actually be complementary, interconnected, and interdependent in the natural world, and how they may give rise to each other as they interrelate to one another.

Yin is feminine (not be mistaken for the female gender) it represents the ever retracting, imploding, receiving, yielding and gentle nature.
Yang is masculine (not to be mistaken for the male gender) ever expanding, exploding, producing energy.

Chi-Gong follows the principle of the Yin and Yang at once, simultaneously in a mindful/mindless play. Bruce Lee said "water can flow or it can crash" "You must be shapeless, formless, like water." "When you pour water in a cup, it becomes the cup. When you pour water in a bottle, it becomes the bottle. When you pour water in a teapot, it becomes the teapot. Become like water my friend."

THE BODY ELECTRIC

As Western chemistry has become more refined, it is now able to demonstrate that our bodies are filled with energy and electric charges. Back in February 1984, an article in Discover magazine by K. C. Cole, explained the comparison:

"Electricity is almost certainly the most elusive of everyday things: It lives in the walls of our houses, and regulates the lives of our cells.... It runs electric trains and human brains.... Your entire body is a giant electric machine: body chemistry (like all chemistry) is based on electrical bonds."

Chinese medicine is based on a person's ability to maintain the proper circulation of this bioelectric energy through the body. If you have ever had acupuncture, you have experienced the circulation of this bioelectric energy, which the Chinese call Chi (pronounced CHEE), in your own body. Not to worry if you have not had the opportunity to feel your Chi before, Chapter 2 is all about you! *smiles*.

The idea of chi is not unique to China. Dr. John Mann and Larry Short, authors of The Body of Light count forty-nine cultures around the world that have a word for chi; the words vary from *Prana* in Sanskrit to *Ashe* in Yoruba to *Neyayoneyah* in Lakota Sioux, are all equivalent terms. In the West, we speak about feeling energised or about having low energy, but with a few notable exceptions, we tend to ignore this important part of our physical body.

The concept of chi is gaining increasing acceptance in the medical establishment. Especially since the world wide pandemic where the wellbeing of employees, children and vulnerable populations has become of high priority. Funded Wellness programmes popping up at all types of work spaces to improve the overall Chi in the atmosphere.

As it relates to Traditions Chinese Medicine being accepted in the West. A major transition occurred when President Richard Nixon re-established diplomatic relations with China in 1972. In Beijing, Chinese doctors performed emergency surgery on New York Times correspondent James Reston, using only acupuncture for anesthesia. Since then, many delegations of Western physicians to China have witnessed similar events. Chi is just beginning to be understood in the terminology of Western science. Furthermore, several Western physicians are exploring the phenomenon, such as Robert Becker, a Syracuse University orthopedist and author of The Body Electric, who is trying to explain chi in relation to his work in bio-electricity and healing. It was Dr. Becker's research into electricity and its role in regenerating bones that led to the current method of using low-level electrical currents to stimulate the mending of fractures.

WHAT DOES ENERGY FEEL LIKE WHEN IT IS MOVING IN YOUR BODY?

The fact is that you already have energy, or chi, moving through every part of your body. Without it, you would not be alive. Generally we just are not aware of this current of energy moving through our bodies. When we first become aware of chi, we may experience many different sensations. Some of the most common that people report are warmth, tingling, prickling (like the feeling of static electricity), pulsating, humming, bubbling, and buzzing. Some people feel it move slowly, while others feel a fast "rush." Though some people feel it move in a straight line along the Microcosmic Orbit, most people feel it more at some points along the orbit than at others.

HOW DOES CHI MOVE?

There is a Taoist saying: "The mind moves and the chi follows." Wherever you focus your attention, the chi tends to gather and increase. As biofeedback experiments have now confirmed, focusing your attention on an area of the body can cause increased activity in the nerves and muscles in that area. The stronger the focus, the greater the movement of the chi. Keep in mind that you are not pushing o pulling the Chi, you are simply shifting your focus to another point. Understanding this is crucial to developing an effective practice. However, you will not just be moving your attention over your skin, you will be experiencing a palpable flow of warm, tingling energy.

YOUR MICRO-COSMIC ORBIT

You have bioelectric energy in every cell of your body. This energy also travels along certain well-defined circuits, called meridians, which acupuncture utilizes to regulate the amount of chi in any particular part of your body. The main circuit in the body is called the Microcosmic Orbit (see figure 3) and is made up of two channels, the Back Channel and the Front Channel (in Chinese medicine traditionally called the Governor Channel and the Functional Channel, respectively). These channels are part of our earliest development. In utero, our body first resembles a flat disk. As the embryo develops, the disk folds over, leaving two seams, one along the midline of the back of our body and one along the front. The back seam can be seen in our spine, but the front line is more subtle. We rarely notice the front seam unless it does not close completely, as is the case with a child who is born with a harelip.

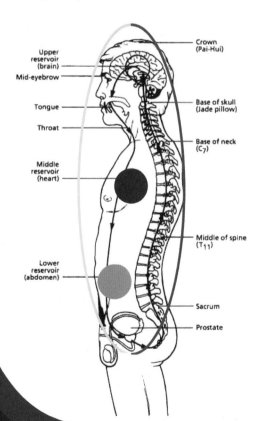

Upper reservoir (brain)
Mid-eyebrow
Tongue
Throat
Middle reservoir (heart)
Lower reservoir (abdomen)

Crown (Pai-Hui)
Base of skull (Jade pillow)
Base of neck (C₇)
Middle of spine (T₁₁)
Sacrum
Prostate

THE BACK CHANNEL

The Back Channel begins at the perineum and runs along the back of the body from the tip of the tailbone, up the spine and neck, to the crown of the head, and finally down the forehead to where it ends between the bottom of the nose and the upper lip, where there is an indentation.

THE FRONT CHANNEL

The Front Channel runs from the tip of your tongue to your throat and along the midline of your body down to your pubis and perineum. Touching your tongue to your palate closes the Microcosmic Orbit. The Front Channel is sometimes translated from the Chinese as the Conception Channel, and if you look very closely at the belly of a woman who is pregnant, you will generally see a dark line (which doctors call the linea nigra) that extends along part of this channel.

CHI-GONG

QI-GONG

CHI-KUNG

SAME SAME
SMALL SMALL

15

CHAPTER 2:

GET STARTED
NOW

VISCERAL VALUE

This chapter is to give you a visceral experience of Chi-gong. You can read all day about energy but the true beauty is taking a moment to feel your own. I provide 2 exercises that you can pause reading and engage in for a few minutes each. The focus here is to give your full attention and presents to these exercises as you are doing them. Be aware of your environment, TV on? turn it off! Mobile phone notifications? Do Not Disturb Mode. In a busy room? remove yourself and enter a quieter space.

I feel you get the idea.

There is a simple
experiment you can do to feel your body's chi:

- Rub your hands together for ten seconds as hard and fast as you can
- Then hold the palms about an inch apart.
- If you concentrate, you should be able to feel a flow of energy passing between them.

FLOAT & DISSOLVING CHI

LEVEL: BEGINNER FRIENDLY

ABOUT

This beginner friendly breathing technique uses the hands as the meditation object. Further bringing the breathe into rhythm & synergy with the hand movements.

"Where your focus goes, energy flows"

STEP 1

Breathe in: starting your hands at the low belly, draw your awareness up as you breathe in and move you hands up.

STEP 2

Breathe out: bring your hand slowly down. Softening your fingers as you dissolve the weight of gravity from your hands, shoulders, neck and jaw through your core and into the floor.

SELF MASSAGE

LEVEL: BEGINNER FRIENDLY

ABOUT
This self massage involves the cervical spine and occipital groove as the focus. This is a key gateway to allow the breath to circulate smoothly around the microcosmic orbit. [See on page 13]

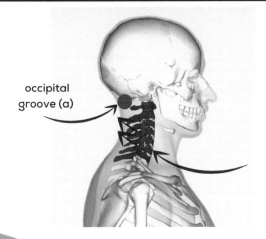

occipital groove (a)

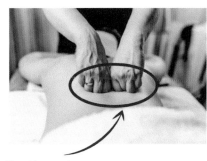

Knuckles as the massage tool (b)

HOW?

STEP 1	Bring your hands to point (a)
STEP 2	Make your knuckles in the shape of (b)
STEP 3	Roll your knuckles side-to-side on the occipital groove
STEP 4	Breath out and release your jaw side-to-side.

DECODING YOUR EXPERIENCE

I am a firm believer in reflecting on our energy experiences to find words that articulate the experience, to get to know the different qualities of our own energy. Maybe, as you read this you are feeling some reasons why that may be useful to you.

Here are some questions to help you articulate what just happened in your body.

Were there any noticeable changes in your heart rate or pace of breath? If yes, what exactly did you notice change?

....

Was the energy you experienced very intense or very subtle?

....

Did any of the exercises leave new sensations in your body? If yes, describe the sensation and where it was located?

....

....

....

THE ART OF APPROPRIATE APPLICATION

CHAPTER 3:

If Chi-gong represents a generalized description of the process gone into building your energy. Essentially you will be plugging yourself into the earth & growing your battery power for higher volts of vibrations. When done with the chest proud & at ease, sometimes one can experience wave patterns and gentle pulses throughout the skeletal structure. High volts aren't to be confused with sharp jolts

This comprehensive training manual represents the way to actualize this process personally. The very essence of Chi-gong lies in the recognition of your own internal climate & adjusting that where necessary, toward the feeling of harmony. Essentially adapting the practice to you as an individual, not adapting the individual to the confines of the practice.

Although community is essential for growth, one of the key insights of Chi-gong is developing a personal practice. A cardinal piece is to respect all our individual situations and requirements. Furthermore, to take into account a persons constitution, place, gender, time, age, capacities, aspirations and activities. In keeping with this insight, its practices are concerned with not only the development of our bodily structure, but of our breath, voice, memory, intellect, character and heart as well.

Although Chi-gong has general principles of movement and breath, your Big Why for practicing Chi-gong will be most necessary for you to identify how to appropriately apply your practice, especially in the beginning stages. I will reveal some approaches to practice and how to apply your "Why" & intentions there. We will cover Your Big Why later in this section and even help you get really clear on it.

FOUNDATION 3
TO FREE YOU CHI

THE ART OF
APPROPRIATE
APPLICATION

3 things are happening
simultaneously in Chi-gong Practice.

MENTAL EXPERIENCE

FEELING EXPERIENCE

MECHANICAL EXPERIENCE

THE BREAKDOWN

Where your focus goes, energy flows.
3 things are happening simultaneously in Chi-gong Practice.
The mental experience, The Feeling experience and the
Mechanical experience. The Mental Experience is about what
you call in, what thoughts are you choosing to recode your
mind with e.g. affirmations of Love, Joy, Peace, Radical Fierce
Freedom. The Feeling Experience is noticing the quality of
sensation present in your body e.g. heat, cold, tingles, softness
etc. The Mechanical experience is your bones alignment as you
unwind into yourself. Your Body-Mechanics will always lean
towards golden ratio, naturally encoded perfection when you
Mental & Feeling in your attentive awareness. Your Physical
body will naturally express these feelings and thoughts in your
movement. It's a challenging act, It's a balancing act. The Truth
is, you've been there before. It's just like riding a bike. Once you
hop on, you'll naturally pick it up. Balance will be natural and
you'll move forward in ease, just like riding a bike again.

THE BIG WHY

The following 3 examples are the Big Why's of practitioners in previous rounds of the Chi-gong for Change Challenge:

Example 1

"I intend to use chigong to feel at ease in my body and peace in my mind."

Example 2

"My goal is to tune up my ability to feel, harness & abundantly harvest energy."

Example 3

"I wish to improve structural integrity and balance in my body with chigong".

The following are how to appropriately apply the Big Whys previously mentioned in practice:

Example 1

During practice you should create a supreme sense of softness throughout the hands & fingers, jaw & tongue.

Example 2

Dedicate 1 month of practice to mastering the fundamentals of Chi-gong Exercise. Including the Phoenix Pose, 8 Treasures/Brocades & 5 Wudang Animals.

Example 3

Dedicate time in the early morning or evening to do Chi-gong Meditation. Focus of building attentive awareness & refine the quality of Chi you feel. Always finish with Dan Tien Breathing to store the energy built

YOUR BIG WHY

This page is full of questions to get you clear about your own practice:

Have you done a Chi-gong class before?

....

What parts of the class did you like? Breathing exercises, warm-ups, games, postures, sensations. Any surprises for you?

....
....

Is there anything you would like to learn more about?

....
....

[TICK ALL THE BOXES THAT RESONATE]
If it were possible for Chigong to help you in your normal daily life,
Where would you want it to help you?

(1) Depression ☐ (2) Stress ☐ (3) Anxiety ☐ (4) Poor Sleep ☐
(5) Brain Fog ☐ (6) repatterning new behaviours ☐
(7) increase endocrine hormone production/energy levels ☐
(8) relieve joint pain/improvement ease in movement ☐
(9) feel presence, move subtle energies ☐
(10) build instinct and intuition ☐

NOW, WHAT IS YOUR BIG WHY?

....
....
....

WELL DONE!

BUT, IF YOU ARE STRUGGLING TO
IDENTIFY YOUR BIG WHY,
SEND AN EMAIL ENTITLED "MY BIG WHY"
TO REES.THE.FLAME@GMAIL.COM

CHAPTER 4:

CHI-GONG FOR HEALING

MY HEALING JOURNEY, REES DUNN

My Journey with Chi-Gong began one day when having an open mind to try a youtube follow along entitled 'Qi-Gong: 7 Minutes of Magic' by Lee Holden. I don't know if magic is what I experience but a new hope was risen within me. Why? I had endured 10 years of tremoring hands due to side effects of pharmaceutical medication for epileptic seizure I was having. Let's rewind 10 years to fast forward.

The seizures began when I was 9, in my sleep. As seizure are involuntary, I went from a child who plays in the mud, climbs trees and rides his bike wherever the wind blows to the overly cradled child who is potentially a hazard if he has an 'episode'. My parents, of course worried and uninformed, were rushed into choosing very strong pharmaceuticals drugs to stabilise the rate in which I was having seizures. The Doctors mentioned side effects may arise. Not long after I began taking the medication daily, which I was on for 6 years straight, I noticed an involuntary quivering in my hands. My Mama noticed, My Friends noticed, My Teachers noticed...Heck! Everybody noticed. I may aswell have had Parkinson's disease, because the side effects of the Meds were so bad! Remember, I am 9, 10, 11 years of age. My Handwriting regressed, reading abilities regressed, belief in my academic abilities plummeted. All because my hands had a tremor they didn't have before.

Fast forward 10 years, I am 19. Working as a Bodyweight Training Coach for the Royal Family of Kuwait and the Diplomatic families living there. I'm doing things none of my peers are doing. My belief in Myself carried me so far so fast. I am strong, young and having the best fun! However, people still notice, I have a constant involuntary quiver in my hands. Not as bad as my school years, however still noticeable. So again, one day when having an open mind to try a YouTube follow along entitled 'Qi-Gong: 7 Minutes of Magic' by Lee Holden. I noticed immediately that my hands were more sturdy. Even after the 7 minutes were over, the sturdiness and calmness in my hands remained. I was astonished at this seem to be miracle at the time. I was also bewildered at how 7 minutes of this Chinese Not-Kung-fu-Kung-fu had settled years of mess in my body, I stayed consistent practicing that video and other Chi-gong videos about 3 times a week at that point. My Tremor reduced intensity by 70%. Then later I discovered this ancient Chinese Physician who I have written a case study around on the next few pages.

MEET THIS GUY, SUN SI-MIAO

Sun Simiao was a Chinese Physician and revolutionary writer, as it relates to sustainability of balance in the multiverse that is, human health. He was even titled as 'China's King of Medicine' for his significant contributions to Chinese medicine and tremendous care to his patients.

THE 13 GHOST POINTS

Sun wrote two books - Beiji Qian Jin Yao Fang ("Essential Formulas for Emergencies [Worth] a Thousand Pieces of Gold") and Qian Jin Yi Fang ("Thousand Ducat Formulas") - that were both milestones in the history of Chinese medicine. The 13 ghost points were introduced by Sun Si-Miao for the treatment of epilepsy, schizophrenia & manic behaviours.

He released this 13 Ghost points at a time when the culture was becoming more advanced and psychological illnesses became more prevalent. He began a systemic approach to the treatment of mental illness ("kuang dian").

When treating mental disorders, a practitioner will use acupuncture points to address the underlying pattern, and ghost points would be added as needed to help ground the person. Alongside receiving treatment from a acupuncturist, anybody can apply acupressure to these points themselves and stimulate the meridians.

This perspective created an "it's possible" mindset for those whose belief in themselves were dampened by society calling them crazy. The 13 Ghost Points to release the "ghosts" that haunt a person prove of great value until today more than 1500 later. These "Ghosts" can include beliefs/thought patterns, bad habits/addictions, and obsessive thoughts/behaviours, etc. Sun Si Miao also mentions that the "Ghosts" affecting the mind is actually excess phlegm misting the Heart mind. As we know excess phlegm can be the result of long standing emotional issues or trauma, weak Jing (Essence), diet, external pathogens, drugs, or shock.

SUMMARY

Sun's 13 Ghost Acupuncture points are significant in the process of healing the trauma on the autonomic nervous system (ANS) that comes after epileptic episodes. My point here is **not** to highlight the 13 ghosts are a cure for epilepsy, schizophrenia and manic behaviour. However, All the Ghost points have applications that affect a patient's emotional and psychological welfare. With consistent use of Acupressure, Chi-Gong & other TCM modalities, there is proof a person can heal the aftermath of psychologically traumatic events and tranquilize the shock, fear, uncertainty, worry that occurs in the body and mind **after** the heightened challenging event.

Furthermore, patients continue to report more and more, even myself, that Chi-Gong & Acupressure when used together they create a sense of peace, help centre and ground them.

Heart Rate Variability

Heart health will always be a priority research for obvious reasons, it being a primary organ for sustaining any animals life. Even Harvard Medical School stated that HRV is the new way of tracking wellbeing. It's particularly interesting as it is a noninvasive way to identify these autonomic nervous system (ANS) imbalances. If a person's system is in more of a fight-or-flight mode, the variation between subsequent heartbeats is low. If one is in a more relaxed state, the variation between beats is high. In other words, the healthier the ANS the faster you are able to switch gears, showing more resilience and flexibility.

There was a study done on elderly people, as it relates to of Chi-gong & HRV. This is because population aging is occurring worldwide, and preventing cardiovascular related events in older people is a unique challenge. The aim of this study was to examine the effects of a 12-week qigong training program on the heart rate variability and peripheral vasomotor response of middle-aged and elderly people in the community. This was a quasi-experimental study that included the pre-test, post-test, and nonequivalent control group designs. Seventy-seven participants (*experimental group* = 47; *control group* = 30) were recruited. The *experimental group* performed 30 min of 'Eight-form moving meditation' 3 times per week for 12 weeks, and the *control group* continued their normal daily activities. After 12 weeks, the interaction effects indicated that compared with the control group, the experimental group exhibited significantly improved heart rate variability and peripheral vasomotor responses.

Furthermore, As a teacher and practitioner of Chi-Gong. I know that the slow-motion movements we do aren't just to dodge bullets in the matrix. They are slow because we are inviting the autonomic nervous system to shift over to a relaxed state. Therefore, of course *experimental group* were going to see significant improvement in HRV upon consistent efforts for 12 weeks, Chi-Gong is for slowing down the rate in which the heart beats.

6 HEALING SOUNDS, SUN SI-MIAO

To celebrate Sun Si-Miao's contribution, here's his well known self healing sound therapy practice. The '6 Healing Sounds', it is a form of vibrational medicine and a health practice. The vibration stems from sounds created by different positions of the mouth and tongue. These various sounds affect different parts of the body, organs, and meridians. The sounds are also related to the seasons. Sun Si-Miao was the first to record these different sound-body-season combinations. The following will give an overview of the six healing sounds and an approximation of what they sound like. If the reader is interested in practicing this art, it would be best to have someone who knows, personally demonstrate the sounds.

1. Su - Sounds like "shhh"
Season - Spring
Organ - Liver (also relates to the eyes)

2. He - Sounds like "huh" or "hurrrr"
Season - Summer
Organ - Heart and Circulatory System
(Also relates to tongue)

3. Hu - Sounds like "whooo"
Season - Occurs between all seasons
Organ - Spleen and systems of digestion

4. SI - Sounds like "ssss" or "zzzz"
Season - Fall
Organ - Lung and Respiritory System
(Also Relates to the nose)

5. Chui - Sounds like "choowee"
Season - Winter
Organ - Kidney and Systems of Elimination and Hormones
(Also relates to the ears)

6. Xi - Sounds like "shee"
Season - Occurs between all seasons
Organ - Triple Burner System - For absorbing energy from food

CHAPTER 5:

ENERGY CENTERS IN CHI-GONG

ENERGY CENTERS IN CHI-GONG

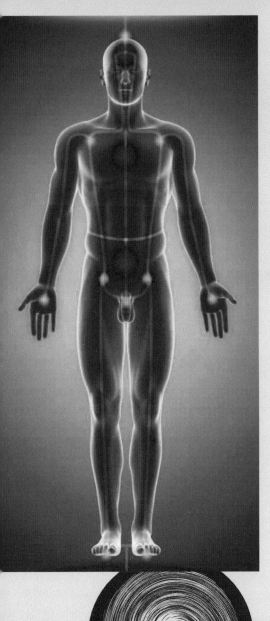

Dan tien or tan t'ien is loosely translated as "elixir field", "sea of qi", or simply "energy center". In Traditional Chinese Medicine (TCM), Dan Tien are considered to be energy centers similar to the Indian yogic concept of Chakras.

They're believed to hold the "three treasures" of the body, known as:

- Jing
- Chi
- Shen

These are thought to be subtle energies that support and sustain the blood, bodily fluids, and solid tissues.
According to tradition, practitioners cultivate and protect the proper formation and circulation of the Dan Tien energies to restore and promote health and well-being. This involves cultivating the qi, or life force, into more rarefied forms.
Dan. Tien are considered by some to be essential for cultivating health and wellness on a subtle level.

They're believed to support the development of the physical body as well as the development of the mind and the soul on the path of consciousness,

Dan Tien are also used in:

- Tai Chi
- Chi Gong
- Reiki
- Kung Fu

In traditional martial arts, proper posture and movement are coordinated with the breath to cultivate energy within the Dan tian centers.

ENERGY CENTERS IN CHI-GONG

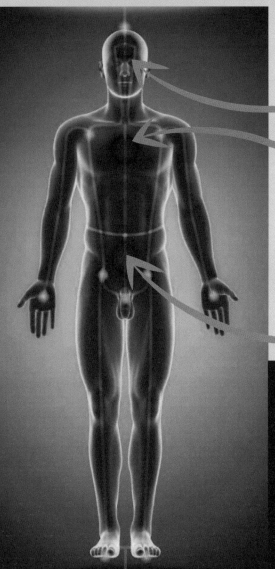

UPPER DAN-TIAN

MIDDLE DAN-TIAN

LOWER DAN-TIAN

All Dan-Tiens & meridian points are accessible to us. "Where your attention goes, energy flows" The Lower Dan-Tien, mentioned above, is the prodominant space to store energy. Acting like your fuel tank. This is why we start, have intervals breaks and finish practice in the lower Dan-Tien awareness.

WHAT ARE THE 5 ANIMALS OF WUDANG?

[2] Tiger

[1] Leopard

[4] Crane

[3] Dragon

[5] Snake

If you want to grow your Yang energy of Chi-Gong discipline, then Wudang Animals are 5 movements that can grow your fortitude, focus and fortune. We have a full video course available for you to access, digest and embody the qualities of these animals/mythological ones too.

Alongside this, the forms will target specific meridian channels and open the so your energy can flow smoothly for joint, blood flow and organ health.

Once you have the mechanics down, you can use them as an empowerment tool to embody the pro-dominant qualities of these animals. We have a full video course available, please visit our website for at
https://betterchigong.education

THE LAYERS OF YOU

CHAPTER 6:

THE LAYERS OF YOU

You are so much deeper than you realise.
This section is about acknowledging the different layers
of who you are. When you practice, if you start to
unpeel these layers like an onion then your body can
begin to open up in new ways and thus you will be
granted the space for more knowledge of self. The
whole process is quite astounding and just like life, is a
journey to be savoured.

THE LAYERS OF YOU:

YOUR 6 BODIES

MENTAL

EMOTIONAL

SPIRITUAL

PHYSICAL

INNER CHILD

PRIMAL

41

THE LAYERS OF YOU:

GIVING ATTENTION TO YOUR 6 BODIES

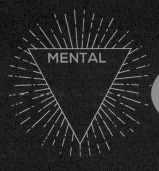

MENTAL

In other words...be aware of the quality of your thoughts while practicing. Are you thinking about lunch later or your to-do list for today? Are you telling your self with empowering affirmations as you breathe? Be aware of this while practicing .

PHYSICAL

In other words...be aware of the quality of Chi in your body today today while practicing & how it changes from the beginning, middle and end of practice. Are you breathing the movements alive? Are you focused on discomfort, pain or irritation in your body? Be aware of this while practicing .

EMOTIONAL

Emotions are simply visitors, they don't own you, they are not you and you are not your emotions. However, all emotions you ever have and ever will experience are valid. As you practicing, ask & be authentic with yourself. How was I feeling before this practice? How do I feel in this now? Just like going for a run, your Chi-gong practice can serve as a way to ground and release heavy emotions. At the end of a practice you can feel a miraculous sense of clarity and contentment in your emotional state, as if you have consciously renewed your own self. Be aware of this while practicing .

GIVING ATTENTION TO YOUR 6 BODIES

SPIRITUAL

We are all spiritual beings living a human experience. Your tender spirit and your warrior spirit are both a matter of your heart space. Your ability to truly know and work yourself is a matter of listening to spiritual messages coming through your own heart.
The root of the word spirit is the latin Spirare which means Breathe. So anything that deepens the breathe will inherently grow the fruits of your spirit. Whether that be laughter, crying, dance, yoga, gardening, a workout or your chi-gong practice, all these things plus more can work your breathe and thereby work your spiritual muscle per say.

INNER CHILD

Chi-gong can be a great way to release trapped emotions. During practice, people often experience moments of bliss, laughter & even tears. after these kinds of sessions, a big weight can be lifted from a person. A weight which sometimes has been around since childhood. If you have a breakthrough like this, you will know & you will be able to move on with your life more content with the past, content with yourself, resent other far less if at all and forgive much easier.
So I prompt you to shamelessly express your feelings as if the child inside you were taking control over you and see the magic that unfolds for you after that.

PRIMAL

Innately, we all have a wild primal side within us. Innately, as children we pretend to be different animals. Innately, we all have animals that call our spirit to feel more empowered.
Beat your chest and raise up your voice, your breath, your movement.
Don't be afraid to celebrate your filthy animal within.

THE LAYERS OF YOU:

JOURNALLING PROMPTS

This page is full of **questions** to assist you in diving you deeper into your relationship with your layers:

Which of the 6 layers mentioned do you feel most close to?

....

What of the 6 layers do you feel most distant from?

....

What is the first distant memory arising when you look at the distant layer?

....

....

Now, create a loving affirmation to nurturingly call that distant layer of yourself closer in?

....

....

Take a deep breath

3

CHAPTER 7:

UNIVERSAL LAWS EXPRESSED IN CHI-GONG

The universe is structured & designed in pure and unarguable math.
Chi-gong is a practice that abides by universal law
and thus this next section will be mathematical.

UNIVERSAL LAWS
EXPRESSED IN CHIGONG:
FIBONACCI SEQUENCE

Fibonnaci AKA the golden ratio, golden mean is the desirable middle between two extremes. Expressed in the pattern of the ever growing spiral. The sequence starts:

0, 1, 1, 2, 3, 5, 8, 13, 21, 34, 55, 89, 144, ...

UNIVERSAL LAWS EXPRESSED IN CHIGONG:

VORTEX MATH

WHAT IS A VORTEX?

The vortex describes an inward contraction with its equal expansion which is the inner form of a torus [1]. Vortex math numbers illustrate the contracting and the expanding elements of the external physical plane and they also illustrate the internal and subtle aspect of consciousness.

Understanding the Pattern

We're going to create a pattern of single-digit numbers using multiples of 2. Take the number 1. Multiply it by 2, and you get 2. Multiple it by 2, and you get 4. Again, you get 8. Again, and you get 16. 16 is two digits, but we only want one-digit numbers, so we add them together, getting 7. Double, you get 14, so add the digits, and you get 5. Double, you get 10, add the digits, and you get 1. So you've got a repeating sequence: 1, 2, 4, 8, 7, 5, ...

Take the numbers 1 through 9, and put them at equal distances around the perimeter of a circle [2]. Draw an arrow from a number to its single-digit double. You end up with something that looks kinda-sorta like the infinity symbol. You can also fit those numbers onto the surface of a torus. The numbers reveal a spiral line and a curved plane.

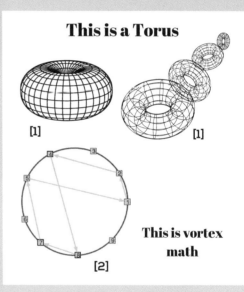

This is a Torus

[1]
[1]

This is vortex math

[2]

According to vortex math, there's something deeply significant about that pattern:

1) If you make metallic windings on a toroidal surface according to that pattern and use it as a generator, it will generate free energy.
2) Take that same coil, and run a current through it, and you have a perfect, reaction-less space drive (called "the flux thruster atom pulsar electrical ventury space time implosion field generator coil").
3) If you use those numbers as a pattern in a medical device, it will cure cancer, as well as every other disease.
4) If you use that numerical pattern, you can devise better compression algorithms that can compress any string of bits.
5) and so on...

UNIVERSAL LAWS EXPRESSED IN CHIGONG:

VORTEX MATH

CONCLUSION:

Essentially, according to vortex math, that repeated pattern of numbers defines a "vortex", which is the deepest structure in the universe, and it's the key to understanding all of math, all of physics, all of metaphysics and all of medicine. It's the fundamental pattern of everything, and as a matter of fact, this equation is the universes way of fitting infinite potential into a finite space. Your body is a finite space within this same infinitesimal wisdom. Chi-gong is a doorway you can walk through to access this dormant energy within you and harness it to the fullest.

UNIVERSAL LAWS EXPRESSED IN CHIGONG:
GRAVITY
(on Earth)

Acceleration of gravity
or
rate of Freefall

$= 9.8 \, m/s^2$

Another undeniable law of the universe. On earth that is to say, the acceleration of gravity upon the centre of any object attracted to the earth at sea level is 9.8 m/s2. We cannot avoid gravity. However when you have a deadline at work that is getting ever closer and you begin to feel your shoulders become heavier. This a time when stress in your body was going against the grain of the law of gravity. But, again, because it is an unarguable law, gravity didn't care and rebounded the pressure. Therefore, leaving your body in a compression-only state. Both expansion & compression need to be happening to achieve a state of Bio-tensegrity (explained later in this chapter)

No need to fear the stressors and pressures in life & no need to fear gravity. Infact in Chi-gong the intention is to no-longer fight gravity but to adopt a friendly relationship with gravity whereby your intent to let go in practice is aided by gravity itself. Practicing in this way makes it very clear to feel negative energy dissolving down and out your human system.

Again, Gravity is the one force that is always there but little discussed in most health & wellness conversations.

100% of the time is an active force on your body. The nature of gravity is an unwavering force! You need to be in harmony with it. If you are not in harmony with this powerful force, your body will corrode and your health is going to have a lot of problems, both now and in the future. It's there when you're born and will be there when you die. It makes all the difference in how you live inside your body.

As it relates to the three previously mentioned universal laws, can you recognise all three in the picture below?

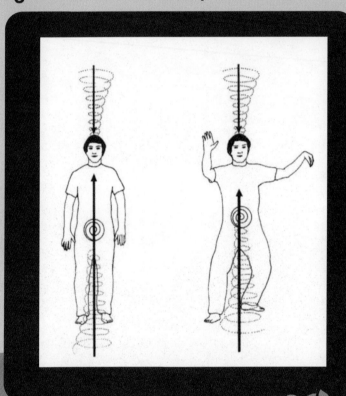

Describe what you recognise...

....

....

....

....

UNIVERSAL LAWS EXPRESSED IN CHIGONG:

GRAVITY SENSING BODY SCAN

EXERCISE:

PART 1: After a few minutes of Dan Tien breathing, you will be intentionally dropping your awareness through specific areas of your body starting at your scalp, let that tension disopate. Allow forehead and eyebrow tension to drop. Allow the eyeballs to drop heavy in the sockets. Allow the tongue to drop heavy in the mouth. Allow the jaw to drop heavy in the neck. Allow the diaphragm to drop from underneath the rib cage. and so on, and so on. until your awareness has dropped into your feet.

PART 2: Although an unusual feeling at first, you want to feel into your bone structure. Start with the major joints in that process. Which is your ankles, knees, hips and then every vertebrae of the spine stacking up on top of one another, opening up the chest and relaxing the shoulders.
(more on how to release yourself from gravity in the Chi-gong4Change).

UNIVERSAL LAWS
EXPRESSED IN CHI-GONG:

LAW OF
RHYTHMN

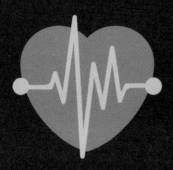

UNIVERSAL LAWS EXPRESSED IN CHI-GONG:

LAW OF RHYTHMN

All natural movement in the universe comes in patterns & rhythmic movement.
As it relates to Chi-Gong, keeping a listening ear open can extremely heighten the senses, which are your super power. Your body responds to sound faster than your body responds to light.
Universally law however, is that the speed of light is faster than the speed of sound.

Why is that? Why does your body respond to sound faster than your body responds to light?

 Well we know our brains are like computers and in this instance, your computer is processing some things faster than others. Auditory stimulus reaches the brain in 8-10 milliseconds, where-as visual stimulus reaches the brain in 20-40milliseconds. Again, even though the speed of light is faster than the speed of sound, your body is receiving these 2 frequencies in reverse.

For example, you are outside a club and someone is entering your personal space and being aggressive. In this instance, the heat in them has rose so high that they choose to swing a punch at you. Your eyes will see their torso twist, shoulder, fist sequentially and respond too late. By the time your eyes figure out what's happening, you would have already been hit by then. However, same scenario but in this instants you were in a listening state, taking in the sounds in the whole environment. Now when a hasty or sudden sound happens, like a shoe squeaking or jacket rustling in rotation, your instinctual reaction time will be a lot more alert, on beat & it may just save your life.

YES YES YES, I am encouraging you to change you perspective. Chuck out the tunnel vision and hazy edges, tight jaw, closed ears. Invite a panoramic view to your vision, a loose tongue/ jaw and a softer listen.

Yes we cultivate peace in Chi-gong. However, peace doesn't mean you are slow with no live-wire. Urgency, alertness, being on beat are just as important. Supreme peace breeds supreme power. Even the birds in the trees are tweeting in supreme peace but they too, have their neck on swivel and will tick-tak-tock their necks in alertness. Supreme peace breeds supreme power YOU WILL FIND YOUR HARMONY IN BETWEEN THE TWO EXTREMES.

DANCE WILL ALWAYS
BE MORE POPULAR
THAN GYM

Dance will always be more popular than gym. Dance involves momentum and your imagination. I don't challenge that gym releases serotonin, although people still feel pain in the gym but we all know, when the music hits you, you don't feel no pain...think about that.

Serotonin & **Dopamine**

are a sweet side effect of rhythmically moving and breathing lighter to music and frankly is unmatched. We even see babies shaking & bouncing their bum-bum joyfully to music...before they can even walk.

Going back to my original statement 'Dance will always be more popular than gym' this is the reason. Gym doesn't give space for the IS-ness. I'm not suggesting that form, structure & scheduling is a bad thing, in fact they are all extremely effective at making progress. The issue with the gym model is that the environment, the movements and even the music isn't in sync with nature. You can spot the natural mover in the gym standing out like a sore thumb. Whether it's the boxer skipping rope, rotating the rope side to side in figure-8's or the kettlebell girl flicking her wrists as she lifts or even the calisthenics guy doing bodyweight exercises. They stick out because your everyday franchise gym is an artificial environment, generally industrialised with no windows and usually not an indoor plant on site.

These practitioners mentioned stick out because they are going with the grain of natural movement patterns, not against it. The grain of natural movement patterns mentioned is the golden ratio AKA the fibonacci spiral, the coil, call it what you like, it's nature's code. This is why movement through music, song and dance are cultural similarities all over the world for as far as humans go back. We have known this.

YES!!! I SAID BONES

Just like in dancing, chi is about your bones being well structured. Bone are the compressive structure of the body, the lasting hundreds and sometimes thousands of years after we a gone.

"Tensegrity", a word coined by Buckminster Fuller to describe a structure whose form relies both on compression and tension. Basically it means, tensional integrity of an architectural structure, statue or in this case, the body. This is where you have compressive elements, ie. the bones. This is also where the suspended parts that are tensional elements, ie. the connective tissue meaning the tendons, ligaments and fascia which suspend and animate. So to be clear, bones DO NOT stack like bricks. They are actually suspended and floating, What this means is that your femur DOES NOT press on your tibia. There is a glassy surface between and it is suspended in a 3-dimension spiralling matrix AKA a Gryoscope.

When you are able to connect the 2 compressive and tensional through the skeletal circuit being activated, it's like BOOM the lights go on, then you have this redistribution of pressure that redistributes the tensional balance throughout your body.

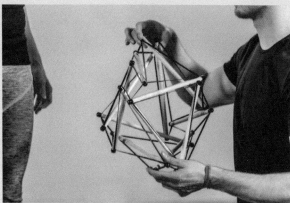

CHAPTER 8:
ROOTING, EARTHING &
GROUNDING

VISCERAL VALUE

THE
COMMON BENEFITS
AMONGST THEIR
SIMILARITIES

ROOTING, EARTHING & GROUNDING!

WHAT & HOW?

The Earth we live on has an electrical charge, this is why life grows up-out of the earth, seen from tropical jungle to volcanoes. The Earth is powerful stuff. Our body can be a conductor of all this power when we get our feet connected. The feet can absorb this energy in the form of negative ions given from the earth up into your body, improving your immunity, cell regeneration, oxygen consumption. Aswell as releasing opposing energy, stress, tension, negative energy in the form of positive ions given from our body back to the earth. It sounds like a fair exchange to me.

WHAT MAKES THEM SIMILAR?

Fundamentally, the common denominator between them all is the connection your feet have to the ground below you and how that energy interacts with the circuits of energy in your body. As it relates to your movement, all 3 have differences in the way to do them to adequately use the grounds energy and force gravity together.
That we will cover together in the next few pages.

- Reduces effects of EMF radiation on your body
- Improves quality of sleep
- Reduces stress & cortisol levels
- Reduces pain & inflammation
- Reduces primary indicators of Oestoporosis
- Improvement of glucose regulation
- Improvement of immune response

WHAT IS THE DIFFERENCE?

ROOTING

Rooting is an active, key word active, internal practice. Whereby the subject stands stationary & stands firm. Often in goat stance or horse stance.

Essentially with any rooting exercise, your imagination should be doing these 3 things:
(1) with your feet, creating roots reaching down deep like a tree.
(2) from tip of your tailbone to the top of your head, creating elongation like you're ringing out a wet towel.
(3) Bamboo legs and arms. Remain strong and durable yet have a sense of feeling elastic with a slight bounce in your arms and legs samely.

EARTHING

Earthing is passive, key word passive, and only requires the resource of a natural element. Essentially, you do not have to do anything for the positive effects of earthing to take place.
What exactly is happening?
Your body is releasing positive ions into the earth and receiving negative ions as fuel from the earth. Negative ions have positive energy and vice versa.

Some examples of earthing:
(1) Picnic in the park on the grass
(2) laying on grass watching the clouds go by
(3) Have a hot bath or soaking feet.

GROUNDING

Grounding is an active, keyword active, external practice with internal alertness. The nature of grounding is more dynamic, easily seen in the following practices/sports:

- Running/Walking
- MMA/Boxing/Other Combat Styles
- All sports where a ball is involved

Essentially, it's all about ground reactive forces e.g. when running and your foot make contact with the floor. How much of the force is being absorbed by the ground? How much of that impact is upshocking back into your body? Is the force transferring organically? thus propelling you into motion or is the force transferring inorganically? thus creating poor patterns of movement that will eventually lead to pain and injury. Learn more at the Chigong4Change group training.

Let's get to the root of it all

ROOTING

"as above, so below"
- Hermes

Starting with the Root. The root chakra is comprised of whatever grounds you to stability in your life. This includes your basic needs such as food, water, shelter, and safety, as well as your more emotional needs such as letting go of fear. When these needs are met, you feel grounded and safe, and you tend to worry less day to day. Balancing the root chakra creates the solid foundation for opening the chakras above. Imagine that you're laying the foundation for a house in which you're going to live for a long time. A solid foundation embedded in firm soil will provide the stability you need to create a home filled with joy for years to come.

Essentially, the physical location of the root chakra is the tailbone & pelvic floor. Many have bruised or bumped their tailbone in early life. Whether this was you or not, most have a frozen tailbone due to sitting for long periods of time. We often don't get to feel the fluid sensation of having a tail often, almost like a Cats or an Eal's. You can liberate the tailbone with an ancient chinese massage, taught by Mantak Chia. (in the next diagram)
This self massage can relieve worry from your life as worry is the fearful opposing emotion to trust.

LVIC MASSAGE

1. Using your fingers, massage your Million-Dollar Point in a circle, first in one direction and then the other.

2. Repeat this massage between your anus and tailbone.

3. Repeat this massage at each of the eight holes of the sacrum. If you can't find the individual holes, massage the general area in several different places, circling first in one direction and then the other.

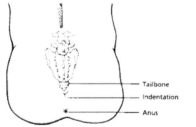

Figure 16 - MASSAGING THE INDENTATION BETWEEN THE TAILBONE AND ANUS

— Tailbone
— Indentation
— Anus

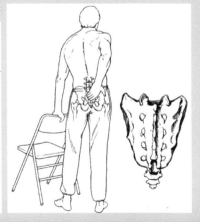

ROOTING IN STATIONARY POSTURES

"Where your attention goes, energy flows"

Within Chi-gong practice, your stationary posture are the main place to focus on Rooting. As displayed in the photo on this page, Tree Posture. These stationary postures are where you really have some moments to feel into which muscles are pegged up in major-minor-tensions. You will have the opportunities to conscious drop that peg and move into deeper grace.

Tree Posture

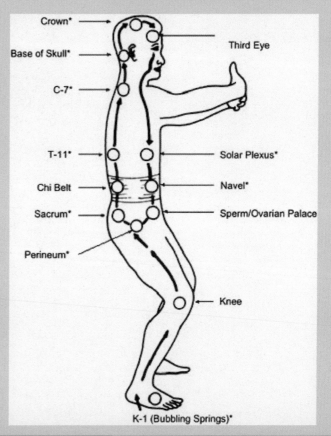

- Crown*
- Base of Skull*
- C-7*
- T-11*
- Chi Belt
- Sacrum*
- Perineum*
- Third Eye
- Solar Plexus*
- Navel*
- Sperm/Ovarian Palace
- Knee
- K-1 (Bubbling Springs)*

Tree Posture
HOW TO HOLD THE ENERGY?

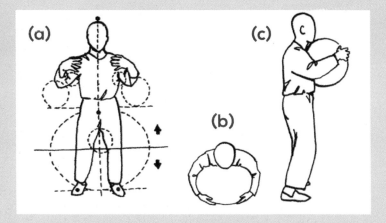

Upon first glance, your body may naturally know what to do with the energy balls shown above. However, I will breakdown them and I will also forewarn that you can interpret these however you want.

We will start at (c) and work our way left.

(c) is a sensation of holding one of those 80s aerobic fitness balls.
(b) is a sensation of hugging someone.

(a) is an extraveganza

Visual examples of

ROOTING

Ever since the lesson with Master Chen Yingjun, I have been practicing tai chi form finding the pressure in the heel first.

Don't try to go low, just try to feel the feet first.

MAJOR KEY:

Visualise the space underneath your feet, as you practice.

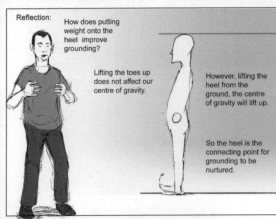

Reflection: How does putting weight onto the heel improve grounding?

Lifting the toes up does not affect our centre of gravity.

However, lifting the heel from the ground, the centre of gravity will lift up.

So the heel is the connecting point for grounding to be nurtured.

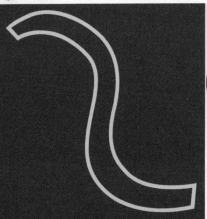

By placing emphasis on bending the knee and not onto the feet creates pain.

Placing emphasis onto the feet, the muscles around the knee will activate naturally.

THE POWER OF PARTNER EXERCISE

Remaining on the topic of grounding and approaching your practice from a different angle is to incorporate your Chi-gong practice with a partner. A true thing of beauty that happens is that your partner just being present, serves as a mirror. We feel the blockage of energy flow because it signals to our body as tension. We are such sensitive beings and you both will be made aware quickly of where you both have resistance. Again, highlighting "where you both a have resistance" because neither is in a position of power in Chi-gong partner training context. Furthermore, it is an experience to release the weight even more from your shoulder and can be used to dust out any energetic impurities or unwanted elements in your own human system.

"Where your attention goes, energy flows".

As you connect with your partner through contact or non-contact partner exercises. Your natural intelligence will detect where the blockage is taking place between you both. Then instead of fighting one another's tension signal with more tension. The aim of the partner training is in fact, to iron out those tense bits until you both can agree, using your natural intelligence, that the energy is flowing smoothly.

If you haven't notice, I'll be clear. Your partners energy is teaching you about your own energy. You are also teaching them about their energy. This equal energy exchanging is good currency.

Leaving a partner practice should feel like your joints & general spring for life has been renewed. Leaving partner practice should not feel like you're more cranked up than before. If so, it means you, being the tenant & controller of your body, were insisting more resistance. Instead of leaning into discomfort. Instead of releasing the neuromuscular holding pattern. Instead of operating in an unrestrained trust with your partner. If you finished more tense that you came in, you are still restrained mentally and of heart. Free your mind, Free your heart. Release expectation, guilt, uncertainty, doubt & preconceived ideas. If this is you, my advice to you is; Surrender. Again, leaning into the discomfort; Surrender. Embrace the vulnerability of connecting with another human being; Surrender. A Famous partner exercise is named Push Hands.

Partner Exercise in Chi-Gong is a type of initiation. To take all negative connotation out of the word initiation in this context. The definition of initiation is "to be introduced to an activity or skill". When practicing with a partner, your body, mind and spirit is downloading epic amounts of information. Your DNA is upgrading. Your neuroplasticity is skyrocketing and your spirit co-ordinates are set more accurately.

A practitioner could follow YouTube videos for 3-4 years and still not grasp what can be downloaded in just 1 partner session. Anyone with an open heart will experience immense benefit from Chi-Gong partner exercise, even if they are not a regular practitioner. Partner practice truly can serve as a milestone on any practitioners journey.

REES

THE FLAME

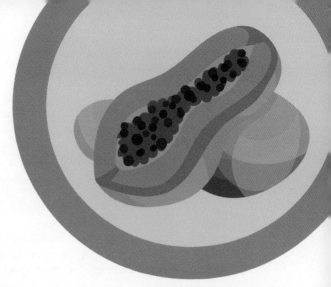

VISCERAL VALUE

CHAPTER 9:
ANATOMY, TECHNIQUES &
BREATH IN CHI-GONG

ABDOMINAL BREATHING
LEVEL: BEGINNER

STEP 1

Recieve your inhale inward and down to to fill your belly big like a balloon. This is your inhale.

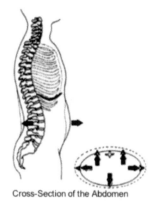

Cross-Section of the Abdomen

STEP 2

Between, take a moment allow gravity to drop from your chest into your belly more.

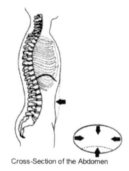

Cross-Section of the Abdomen

STEP 3

Release your exhale and pull your belly button inside.

REVERSE BREATHING
LEVEL: INTERMEDIATE

STEP 1

Recieve your inhale inward and upward big and round in your rib cage. like a free diver would fill his lungs before deep diver into the ocean. This is your inhale.

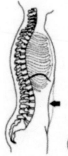

Cross-Section of the Abdomen

(b) Reverse Breathing

STEP 2

Between, take a moment allow gravity to drop from your head top, melting down your face, tongue and jaw.

STEP 3

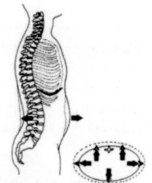

Cross-Section of the Abdomen

Release your exhale down and round out your belly as if you are bloated.

FLOAT & DISSOLVING CHI
LEVEL: BEGINNER FRIENDLY

ABOUT
This beginner friendly breathing technique uses the hands as the meditation object. Further bringing the breathe into rhythm & synergy with the hand movements.

STEP 1

Breathe in: starting your hands at the low belly, draw your awareness up as you breathe in and move you hands up.

STEP 2

Breathe out: bring your hand slowly down. Softening your fingers as you dissolve the weight of gravity from your hands, shoulders, neck and jaw through your core and into the floor.

PACKING CHI
LEVEL: ADVANCED

CHI-GONG
BREATHING
TECHNIQUES

ABOUT

Packing the chi is how many practitioner increase the potency of their chi, martial abilities and become more pillared in their being. When packing the Chi is developed, this where you begin to see people performing greater feats of human capabilities e.g. breaking bricks, bending metal etc.

The technique is an exact fusion of the previous reverse breathing technique combine with the floating and dissolving Chi breathing Technique.

STEP 1

Breathe in: starting your hands at the low belly, draw your awareness up as you breathe in and move you hands up.

STEP 2

Breathe out: bring your hand slowly down. Softening your fingers as you dissolve the weight of gravity from your hands, shoulders, neck and jaw through your core and into the floor.

ABOUT
In chapter 5. Energy Centres in Chi-gong, you learned the 3 Dan Tiens which are located inside the physical body. This page is dedicated to the energy centres connected to your middle and upper Dan-Tien that are outside of your body. Note common colloquial phrases like, "I laughed my head of last night"

CHI-GONG BREATHING TECHNIQUES

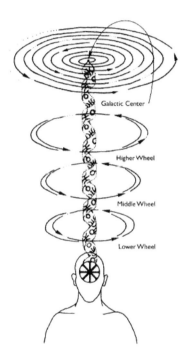

Figure 18. *The upper dimensions of the crown chakra*

Galactic Center

Higher Wheel

Middle Wheel

Lower Wheel

HOW???

These following energy looping exercises will assist you in connecting to and opening the upper dimensions of your crown chakra and start consciously spinning those wheels.
Step 1: Chose 1 colour only from the 3 cycles indicated below.
Step 2a: Sit in meditation in a breathing cycle of your choice
Step 2b: Sync your breath into the chi cycle using your hands to draw the loop.

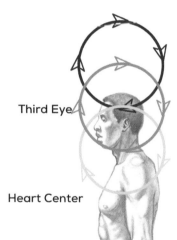

Middle Wheel

Lower Wheel

Third Eye

Upper Dan Tien

Throat Center

Middle Dan Tien

Heart Center

○ Heart to Third Eye Loop

○ Throat to Lower Wheel Loop

○ Third Eye to Middle Wheel Loop

VISCERAL VALUE

CHAPTER 10: ACUPRESSURE, TONING & SOUND

SELF MASSAGE
LEVEL: BEGINNER FRIENDLY

ABOUT

This self massage involves the cervical spine and occipital groove as the focus. This is a key gateway to allow the breath to circulate smoothly around the microcosmic orbit. [See on page 13]

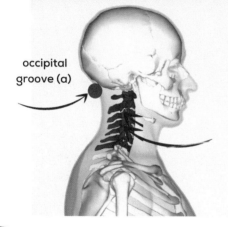

occipital groove (a)

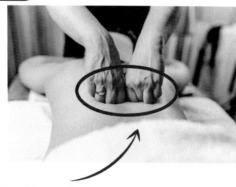

Knuckles as the massage tool (b)

HOW?

STEP 1	Bring your hands to point (a)
STEP 2	Make your knuckles in the shape of (b)
STEP 3	Roll your knuckle side-to-side on the occipital groove
STEP 4	Breath out and release your jaw side-to-side.

SELF MASSAGE
LEVEL: BEGINNER FRIENDLY

TIPS FOR CLEAR FLOWING ENERGY

Meridian points for longevity and good blood circulation.

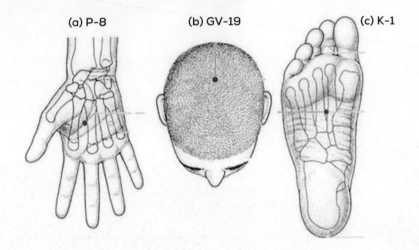

(a) P-8   (b) GV-19   (c) K-1

You're receiving codes about your meridian system just by seeing these 3 points. By simply tapping, circular massage and even breathing life into these points when you train. You can also use a tennis ball or golf ball to roll out the P-8 & K-1 points. Tennis ball is lower intensity. Golf Ball is high intensity which will be very precise and accurate.

KEY:
(a) Pericardium 8
(b) Governing Vessel 19
(c) Kidney 1

WHAT IS TAPPING?

Tapping Is a subsection of chi-gong practice. Tapping is a way of exploring your body, everywhere you can think of. It will awaken your energy and clear stagnant Chi.

HOW DO YOU WANT TO TAP?

Personally, i like the slap and slide. Kind of like when you put on lotion.

SLAP & SLIDE

Predominantly it is YOU. Who decides how you want to touch your skin. Here is some creative suggestions for you to mimic:

LIGHT LIKE A HANDFUL OF SUDS

FIRM & ROUND LIKE KNEADING DOUGH

MORE EXAMPLES ON
NEXT PAGE

JUST LIKE
CLUTCHED ONTO A TEA CUP
TRIPLE SENSATION
SOFT, COMPACT & WARM

THE ART OF
TAPPING

KNITTING NIBBLERS
THESE ARE LIKE KITTY PAWS

"Tapping is reassuring and made me comfortable to release those emotions"
- Tracy, Manifestation Teacher/ Chi-Gong Client

SPOILT FOR CHOICE
TRY THEM ALL & SEE
WHAT WORKS
FOR YOU

HOW DO YOU WANT TO
TAP YOURSELF

 TRY THEM ALL
& SEE WHAT
WORKS FOR YOU

WHAT IS
NEURO-ACOUSTICS?

Neuro-acoustics is utllising the sound of your voice to effect the way you feel in your body. In the Chi-gong community, it is also known as Toning the energy & is a whole subsection of Chi-gong practice. A good place for anybody to start with neuro-acoustics is to make a long hummmm and feel how that permeates through your body.

Try this now
Breathe all the way out, to start
Breathe all the way in
Swallow and hmmmmm [as long as you can]
Do you hear and feel the sound permeate in your ear drums? your neck shoulders, chest, belly etc.
Send the sound all around.
[VISCERAL VALUE]

Why it's called Neuro-acoustics is because each neuron is a nerve for the cells of your body. Each nerve is connected to the whole, Nervous System.

Let's view your nervous system as having 2 modes.
(1) Fight or flight & (2) Resting Easy

Most people are operating in low level panic majority of their day, whether knowing it or not but they hummmmm, the body will recognise the visceral experience and reference it to safety. Which basically is hacking into your nervous system, reprogramming your neurons to happiness and health via the visceral experience of the acoustics from your own voice. "WHAT A WOW!"

& when coupled with Tapping. Neuro-acoustic + Tapping is a healing-health sandwich.

CHAPTER 11

ADVANCING YOUR CHI-GONG PRACTICE

+

Q&A

WHEN SHOULD I PRACTICE OUTDOORS?

THE SIMPLE ANSWER IS
ALWAYS

Due to the elemental factor of being outdoors. i.e. the wind on blowing, the direct connection to the absolute ground circuit, the trees, sky and ambience of birds. Your outdoor practice will always always always recalibrate & re-align you toward harmony, even if you are practicing in something as extreme snow.

However, there are some finer details that come into play with Chi-Gong and outdoor practice.

GIVE THE SUN YOUR BACK

Most often throughout the daylight time, facing your back to the sun when practicing outdoors will be your best option. Fundamentally this back to the sun training allows your sight to take in your whole environment and stops the problem of squinting while training. This is an important factor because Chi-gong is an open eyes meditation. If you do shut your eyes to feel inward while practicing, when you open them, you will see all the magnificence in which the sun is brings light to. Plus in vivid detail you get to see the infinite fractals of creation in which the one Sun shines unto. It's like a HD 4K movie **BUT** with your own eyes.

WHAT IS FORMLESS-FORM?

THE SIMPLE ANSWER IS

FREE FORM MOVEMENT

Essentially, formless form is when you begin to move your body according to your attention staying on the chi-flow as your primary focus. This means you deviating in and out of traditional movements you know alongside movements and hand positions you may create in the moment.

Formless form is an important part of your chi-gong practice. There are things that need to channel through you for you to move forward. So take some moments during your practice to let your movements freely form. Just like you do not tell a tree which way it's branches should grow, neither should you always stick to the strict forms you know. Frankly once you know the forms and they have provided you good structural integrity during movement.

surrender to the Chi and allow the soft pull of it to teach you, surrender to be guided to the truth that is waiting for you.

WHAT IS THE MOST EFFECT WAY TO STAY IN FLOW ALL DAY?

PRACTICE MAKES PROGRESS

Practice doesn't make perfect. Practice makes progress. Integrating Chi-Gong as a practice tool can be useful to remind you where the evergreen, ever flowing, ever burning source of energy is within you. Incorporate it into everything you do and everything you do will cooperate with you. In one of the Chigong4Change Group Trainings, we began incorporating Chi-snacks throughout the day because some of the students were beating themselves up mentally for not having a workout style practice daily and recognised they felt better when they did practice. As Mark Wynter Says, "If you've only got 5 minutes to spare, don't despair!" and so we filled those moments throughout the day with a simple recentering of our Chi. Using whatever movement(s) felt natural in that moment. As Ben Houston would call it, Intuitive Chi-Gong. All as a reminder of where that energy is naturally flowing and giving a moment for you conscious awareness to jump on, line up and remember how to ride that wave. After practicing with this group, Chi-snacks more often throughout the day brought more people closer to sustained equilibrium than 20 minute to 1hr sessions once a day did. So Tap-in to your Chi-Snacks, you only have to have 3 things. Your hands, Your Breathing and Your Attention on synchronising them. 3 things only and you will find synergy in 3 breaths only. Activate your Chi-snack in the elevator, in the shower, when the traffic light is red, if you get light headed from standing up too quickly, to bring your heart rate down after cardio...There are literally so many slots in your day that you deserve to grant yourself access to the remembrance of the location and sensation of your flow state.
That is in the NOW.

OUR MISSION:

MAKING CHI-GONG
RELATABLE, ACCESSIBLE & DIGESTABLE

BETTER CHI-GONG EDUCATION

21ST CENTURY PEOPLE MAKING ANCIENT
GEMS USEFUL FOR 21ST CENTURY PEOPLE

WANT TO EXTEND YOUR EDUCATION?

ONLINE VIDEO COURSES **ON-DEMAND**

INVEST INTO 1:1 COACHING **WITH REES**

JOIN A GROUP TRAINING #CHIGONGFORCHANGE

FREE CONTENT ON YOUTUBE

TO EXTEND YOUR EDUCATION
SEND AN EMAIL OR DM SAYING
'I WANT TO DIVE DEEPER #BETTERCHIGONGEDU'

FOLLOWING WITH ONE OR MORE OF THE 4
EDUCATIONS OPTIONS ABOVE THAT YOU RESONATE
WITH NEEDING RIGHT NOW.

 REES.THE.FLAME@GMAIL.COM

 @REES.THE.FLAME

BETTER CHI-GONG EDUCATION.

21ST CENTURY PEOPLE MAKING ANCIENT GEMS USEFUL FOR 21ST CENTURY PEOPLE

JOIN THE **BETTER CHI-GONG EDUCATION CENTER** & BECOME THE FULLY EMBODIED PRACTITIONER YOU'VE ALWAYS DREAMED

IF YOU'VE ALWAYS DREAMED OF HAVING RAZOR SHARP FOCUS, LONG ATTENTION SPAN OR BEING SUPREMELY AND DIVINELY CONNECTED TO NATURE THEN YOU HAVE COME TO THE RIGHT PLACE.

THOUSANDS OF PEOPLE HAVE RELIED ON REES' COACHING FOR THE GUIDANCE, TOOLS AND RESOURCES NEEDED TO TAKE THEIR HEALTH, THEIR MENTAL, EMOTIONAL AND SPIRITUAL PRACTICE TO A HIGHER PLACE FASTER THAN EVER IMAGINED.

FROM IMPROVED HAPPINESS TO DEEPER BREATHS OR EVEN SENSING SHARPER WITH PINPOINT ACCURACY TO THE SKILLS TO TRANSMUTE NEGATIVITY INTO POSITIVITY. WHATEVER YOUR INTENTION, OUR COURSES AND COACHING SERVICES CAN HELP YOU.

WWW.BETTERCHIGONG.EDUCATION.COM

 REES.THE.FLAME@GMAIL.COM

 @REES.THE.FLAME

BETTER CHI-GONG EDUCATION
21ST CENTURY PEOPLE MAKING ANCIENT GEMS USEFUL FOR 21ST CENTURY PEOPLE

THANKYOU

LEAVE US REVIEW

REES.THE.FLAME@GMAIL.COM

BETTER CHI-GONG EDUCATION

21ST CENTURY PEOPLE MAKING ANCIENT GEMS USEFUL FOR 21ST CENTURY PEOPLE

Printed in Great Britain
by Amazon

12390914R00051